TALES OF A MAD HATTER

A BIPOLAR MEMOIR

Jan Paez

Copyright © 2021 Jan Paez
All Rights Reserved

This book is dedicated to the millions of people who suffer from and struggle with mental illness. I stand with you...

"It's very, very important to know that you are braver than you believe, stronger than you seem, and smarter than you think."
- Christopher Robin

Table of Contents

SEPT 2009: 1
The Beginning: 4
138th St Harlem, New York-1988 6
P.S. 75 10
ECUADOR 19
MOVING 24
BOULDER 26
NORWOOD 98-02' 35
SOPHOMORE YEAR 44
LATIN CLASS AT NORWOOD HIGH 47
Osei and TJ 51
DRIVERS ED AND FIRST CAR 56
FOOTBALL CAMP and NHEC 59
FOOTBALL CAMP 61
JUNIOR YEAR G/F 63
JUNIOR YEAR 66
ESCOBAR WANNABEES 69
RELAY FOR LIFE 73
MEET THE DEVIL 74
SENIOR PARTY 77
LOSING MY VIRGINITY 80
SENIOR CLASS TRIP: MONTREAL 82
RACIST MATH TEACHER 85

PROM 2002	87
FRESHMAN YEAR @ BSC SEPTEMBER 2002	89
SOPHOMORE SEMESTER @ BSC: LOSIN IT	111
2004 Bunker Hill	122
VW GALLERY AND BJS	124
2006 Northeastern University	134
ANETTE 2006	137
NEU	138
Brookline	142
MAY 2008	151
SEPT 2008	154
2009	159
JANUARY 2010	166
Marriage goes South	181
Bar Hopping in NYC	186
West Virginia-Bar Pop Champagne 2012	188
2012 Vegas Trip	190
BOSTON LIFE	193
GRAD SCHOOL 2015	199
MASTER SPLINTER AND HIS FRIENDS 2015-2017	202
December 2016	205
SSU 2016 and Field Education Dept/Internship/CSR	213
SEPT 2017-LEAVING SALEM STATE	218
DIVORCE-APRIL 2019	220
ERIKA	224
PABLO AND NEPHEWS 2019	228

HEART OF GOLD, TROUBLED MIND...230
PANDEMIC 2020..234
HOUSING IN YARMOUTH MAY 2020..236
MCLEAN DETOX..238
PRESENT DAY..240

SEPT 2009:

I threw a bottle of beer through the Grand Canal Pub's window tonight. What is wrong with me? My brother Pablo and his Russian friend Sergei had dared me. You see, we had all been kicked out after some heavy drinking and I was already depressed and angered by the loss of Jeannette. Oh yeah, that's over. I will tell you all about it. But first, back to this story. I guess I was feeling angry, resentful and depressed—you name it, I was feeling it. Pablo desperately wanted to smash the window of the bar in order to get his revenge for the bouncers dragging us out at 2AM. So what did I do? On the count of three we were all supposed to smash the window. One, two, three... and guess what? I was the only one who did it. I think I did it out of sheer loyalty to my brother. I threw the Budweiser bottle, and watched as it smashed a large portion of the glass. I was excited, and full of adrenaline so I started to run fast toward the Haymarket subway station. As I ran down the stairs, I noticed that the large entry gate to the station was locked. I was fucked. It was at this time I noticed that my hand was bleeding profusely. I was numb to the pain because of all of the alcohol I had consumed.

After about thirty seconds, six bouncers rushed to get me, plus the owner of the bar. They grabbed me, the owner got in a couple of kicks, and I felt humiliated as fuck. They walked me back to the bar, and sat me down in front, blood was flowing from my right hand like a goddamn chocolate fountain.

After about ten minutes, I started to feel the pain. I yelled, "My fucking hand hurts." One tough guy bouncer just looked at me and replied, "I don't fucking care. Where are your friends now?" I replied "I don't know," not even fully realizing that they had abandoned me. After about ten more minutes, the Boston Police showed up. Then it hit me like a ton of bricks: What had I done? This wasn't who I was.

At heart I am a good person. I don't cause harm or harbor malice towards anyone. So, when I heard the policed officers asking the owner if he wanted to press charges, I went up to him and began crying, telling him how sorry I was. The owner must have felt some compassion, because he told the cops, "No, I'm not gonna press charges."

Next thing I know, an ambulance had come, and they were taking me to MGH (Mass General Hospital). I cried, in a drunken stupor, throughout the entire ride. They had a hard time wrapping up my bloodied right hand.

When I arrived at MGH, I was still absolutely obliterated. I went into the bathroom and managed to pour blood all over the walls, the bathroom sink, and the floor. The janitor was pissed. The doctor scolded me for this, but I felt like they should've just taken me in instead of leaving me there to wander the halls.

A young surgeon told me that the glass had cut me pretty deep in some parts of my hand, and that I would need fifteen stiches. She shot some kind of medicine into my hand to numb me and then began to sew me up. She me she went to Harvard, but I didn't believe her. I gave her a hard time about it, saying there was no way she had gone there. It obviously upset her. I told her that I was about to start my new job at Harvard School of Dental Medicine, and she told me that I needed to make better decisions or else I was gonna end up in jail.

Pablo and his Sergei had shown up by this point, and drove me home. I have a lot of think about. Like, what would have happened if I'd been arrested and sent to jail? When I got home, I was ashamed to show my father my hand. We just looked at each other; I knew I had let him down. He didn't have to say anything.

I am back to living with my parents, in West Roxbury. Jeannette broke up with me, and after tonight, I feel like a complete and utter failure. We were together for three years. We even bought that nice two family home in Stoneham. I gave her ten grand towards the down-payment on the house. I feel a bit used, to be honest. I am definitely angry. I feel like none of this should have happened. As I sat in the living room, I began crying uncontrollably. For one of the only times in my life, my father attempted to console me. His words to me were: "Jasio, she wasn't the right woman for you." I felt a little better after this. I waited until my father went to bed, and started writing the whole thing down. It always makes me feel a little better to write about all of this shit.

The Beginning:

My story begins in a small town in Lodz, Poland, where my mother Margaret gave birth to me. My mother is Polish and Juan, my father, is Ecuadorian, so I am a mix—this has always led to an identity crisis for me, because I've always felt that I'm not Hispanic enough to fit in with other Latinos, and too Hispanic-looking to fit in with other Polish people. Anyway, I was born in Lodz on May 6th, 1984. From what I have been told, my father couldn't stay in the country, and we left for Hagen, Germany as soon as I was born. I feel it's important to note that my maternal grandmother was schizophrenic. My mother had a difficult upbringing because she had to learn to take care of herself as well as her mother. My grandmother had a lot of auditory hallucinations. She would think that people were spying on her, that she heard them talking to her through the walls, or that they were listening to her conversations over the phone. My grandmother couldn't hold down a job. Back then in Poland, many people didn't understand mental illness, so they just brushed off my grandmother's behavior as laziness and said that she didn't want to work. Meanwhile, my mother would work a few part-time jobs to help support my grandmother and her, and she'd eat meals at other relatives' homes.

One of my earliest memories of living in Germany was that I would often get angry when she neglected me and ignored me for my father. I wanted her to play with me, but she was drinking tea with my father. Because of this, I would become upset, and begin throwing toy cars out the balcony to show that I was angry. There was a competition for my mother's attention between my father and I, and I resented him for it. I remember swallowing a bottle of cough syrup one day and I had to be rushed to the hospital in an ambulance. I was only about three years old. Another time, when my father and I were playing soccer, I stepped on the ball and fell forward, breaking my right wrist. I remember that when I was a child I was sheltered from the world, I didn't have any friends until my brother Pablo was born in 1986. It felt so good to have a new addition to the family. Before I knew it, we had moved to New York City in 1988, when I was only four years old.

138th St Harlem, New York-1988

When we arrived in New York City, Harlem to be exact- we stayed at my paternal grandmother or my "abuelita's" apartment tenement at first. My brother Pablo, my mother and father and I slept cramped in one room in the hot summer humidity. For the first couple of months we stayed there, it wasn't easy. My father enrolled in the City College of New York to study chemical engineering. My mother began taking ESL classes at the Riverside church. It was extremely difficult for us. Eventually, my mother got a job at Riverside Church as an administrative assistant. She made $14,000 for the four of us. Now if you have ever been poor, then you'll know how damn expensive it really is. I absolutely hated it. We wore hand me down clothing, and ate on the cheap whenever we could. We often had a Whopper from Burger King when it was on sale for 99 cents or something from McDonalds on 125th Street. During our earliest years, money was hard to come by. My parents did what they could. My father worked several odd jobs, for instance as an elevator maintenance man, but he ended up injuring his hand and leaving that job. My mother continued to work at Riverside Church, while my brother, who was now almost three years old, began to go to a nursery school. I couldn't go to kindergarten for another year. These were extremely difficult times for me, because my father would leave me at our Super's apartment while he studied or worked. The Super spoke no English, so I couldn't talk to anyone. He would just leave me on the couch all day with the TV on, and I hated it. Not only was I bored, but I felt it was a barrier to me developing socially.

When I finally went to kindergarten, the fact that I couldn't speak a word of English also made things difficult. I would get made fun of by others, even though I tried to play and fit in. It was hard, man. I remember one time, I followed a friend from our kindergarten (which was in the projects) to his house. They took the elevator up and I began to cry because I was lost and didn't know which way to go. Eventually an older black gentleman found me: he took me to a room where I waited until my mother and the kindergarten teacher picked me up. Oh boy, was I in trouble! This was the first time I remember thinking that it was the last time that I would ever spend with my family again. The worst part about it was when that, as were walking home, my mother told me that my father wasn't happy—well she wasn't lying. Whenever my father was home it was like you were walking on egg shells. You had to be extremely quiet as you never knew what kind of mood he was in. Anyway, when we opened the door, everything was quiet. We walked down the long corridor and took a right into the living room next to the kitchen. All of a sudden, my father came out, and he started yelling in Polish and whipping me with his belt. He told me not to ever do that again. As the years went by I began to believe the things that he told me, like what a stupid worthless piece of shit I was. I almost came to feel like I deserved the beatings he gave me. I'll never forget the time when my father took me to C-Town, on 135th Street. -I was seriously hyper when I was a child, and he couldn't handle it so he punched me in the chest. I began crying, as well as hyperventilating. When he noticed the tears rolling down my cheeks he quickly began to apologize. He raised my arms in the air and told me to breathe. I calmed after down a few minutes, but I'll never forget the way he treated me.

My abuelita (grandmother) hooked us up with an apartment on the 3rd floor of our tenement, at 603 W. 138th Street. It had four rooms and narrow long corridors. I'll never forget the roaches and rats, and how my father would kill the rats. He would catch them on a sticky trap; then he had this long stick with a sharp chopping block at the end which he used to cut the rat in half. We would be terrified of this as kids, and would hold onto our mother as he threw the rat out of the window. We had a small kitchen, then there was the living room, my parents' bedroom, and mine and my brother's room at the end of the hallway. There were crackheads all around selling everything from broken VCRs to used shoes—really anything they could get their hands on. We were scared because the front door wasn't very strong, until my father had it replaced with a black steel door. We had more than enough space in that apartment, and my father even rented a room to a local café worker named Humberto, who was also Ecuadorian and always let us borrow his horror movies.

Harlem was a beautiful place—sure there were Dominican drug dealers and Ferraris with crack attached inside the rims, and we did see a bodega store owner murdered, but it was a special place, a place like no other in the world. On a hot summer night, after walking to downtown Manhattan, we would finally come home to Uptown and on our street you could hear merengue music playing, see men playing dominos, and smell the Hudson River and fried Dominican food fresh out of the oven,- And of course there was the "helado" man selling his cherry and coconut ice cream for 25 cents.

Nowadays Harlem has changed a lot due to the gentrification, but the old Harlem of my childhood during the late 80's and 90's will always be very special to me, a place like no other and one that I'm very fond of.

P.S. 75

When I was six years old my mother enrolled me in P.S. 75, on West 96th Street. My first grade teacher was Ms. Wilson; she told my parents that she thought I was deaf because, when she called me by my name, I never answered. Well, I couldn't understand her accent. But most importantly, there was an Asian girl named Jan-Phen, so it was difficult to know which person she was calling. So I had all sorts of hearing testing done and it came out fine—I wasn't deaf, I just couldn't speak English. I took it upon myself to learn to speak and read, thanks to Mr. Ricardo, who was an assistant teacher there from the Dominican Republic. I remember he read to me until I learned to sound out the vowels of the word and began to read to him. We started with very easy basic books such as The Purple People Eater series and went on to more advanced ones. Wherever he is now, I just want to thank Mr. Ricardo, for he was the one that taught me to read.

In second grade I had Ms. Jaro, who I had a huge crush on. She was absolutely beautiful, with a great smile and long black hair. Anyway, I began by helping her after school, cleaning the guinea pig cage and feeding the salamanders. One day, when I was feeding the salamander, I remember taking the rock inside the tank and smashing it. I knew that something wasn't right with me. I also had a problem with hoarding pencils. I never wanted to run out of pencils, so I would hoard them all in my cubby. One day, Ms. Jaro had everyone clean out their cubbies because she wanted to figure out where all the pencils were, and wouldn't you know it—when it came my turn to take my things out of my cubby there were about twenty pencils and I got yelled at. I didn't like when someone yelled at me, it would make me blush beet red and give me panic attacks from a young age. But still, I was infatuated with Ms. Jaro and when I was playing a piano concert at Bloomingdales House of Music I made sure to invite her to come out and see my play. (My mother had signed me up to take piano lessons—I played for 4 years and can't remember how to play anything!). She did come, and I loved every minute of the attention she was giving me. I displayed signs of social anxiety from a young age, but in order to avoid other classmates I would write—a lot. Ms. Jaro said that in the future she would be walking by Barnes and Noble and she'd see my work published. Writing was my gift-and also art—I loved them both. When I was in the 3rd and 4th grades, I would read my stories to everyone, and my paintings would win art awards—I got one that was contested among all the public schools of New York City District. But I had a problem with rage and sitting still. One day my mother and I went to an award show where my work was displayed on the wall. I remember I didn't want to wait and demanded that she take off the painting and take it home with us. She eventually caved in and let me take the painting home. I took it right off the wall because I wanted it. Teachers had no clue that I was angry because I was so shy. I was also terrified of my father, and that was another reason. I can tell you about another time when we went to Teachers' College and my brother and I were swinging on the bathroom stalls. Well, when I was swinging on them, I broke the stall from the ceiling and everything came crashing down. My brother Pablo and I ran out and told our mother, then we all ran out of the college. Another example of my rage was when my mother couldn't afford to get us toys like the Teenage Mutant Ninja Turtles and GI Joe action figures, and it really bothered me. I stole a classmate's Michelangelo figure just because I wanted one so bad. And one day, we were walking home on 135th Street and Broadway, when I wanted a toy gun, but my mother couldn't afford to buy one. I threw a temper tantrum, but she walked out of the store, so I started crying and was yelling and crying until the store owner just gave me the toy gun. I felt so good about that on the way home. This wasn't the first time I had lost my temper and lashed out at my mother—for instance, I remember another time when I was demanding Jolly Ranchers after school.

In 4th grade we had Ms. Selig, who was a very serious by-the-books teacher and seemed to have taken a liking to me. She had split up the class up into smart and not so smart kids. I was in the smart section, so we had textbooks and we did more advanced math and reading, while the other kids didn't get textbooks and often had to share them. I realize that this wasn't fair at all, but at the time, what could I do? At least it felt good to be labeled as the smart kid.

But I had demons in me. Maybe it was because I wanted the attention and love from my father that he wasn't giving me at home. Everyone initially perceived me as this nice quiet good boy but that wasn't the case at all. One day at recess, we were outside playing. I went up to another boy and punched him in the mouth because he had pushed me. I would also often be defending my brother Pablo from the other kids in the playground.

The worst incident was when some white kids were playing and wouldn't allow me to play with them. I'll never forget that day. They said something "like we don't want to play with you, go away". So, when lunch was over, and everyone was walking back to their classrooms, I ran up to the kid that had told me this and punched him hard in the mouth. He began bleeding and I ran away. They never caught me for that because we were in different classes, but that feeling of not being included really bothered me, I was angry inside. Kids in schools can be mean when you don't speak the language and are trying hard to fit in.

My brother Pablo and I would also fight a lot. It wasn't normal. Once we were in the auditorium of our school and, after a drama performance when everyone was getting up, my brother and I began lashing out and punching each other. Others in the audience tried to stop us and began yelling at us. Fuck them! I thought, these uppity white people need to leave us alone and mind their own business. Another time I remember my brother took a kid's leather coat and dumped it in a bucket full of milk and ruined it. The kid's parents demanded that we pay for it, but we just couldn't afford to. My poor mother didn't know what to do. What's a kid in elementary school doing wearing a leather coat to school anyway?

Another time my abuelita knew that I wanted the Super Soaker water gun that had come out. I couldn't buy it at the toy store because it was $15 and I only had a $5 bill. Anyway, abuelita came and got the gun and I thought it was a present. I was so ecstatic that she had got it for me, but then, all of a sudden, she said "Jasio, give me $15 for the water gun." I began to cry and pleaded with her to give me the Super Soaker, telling her that I only had a $5 bill. But she never did. This was also when I began to realize that you need money in this world.

I played basketball in my young days both on teams and recreationally. When Riverbank State Park opened up, thanks to Mayor

Dinkins, the aim was to keep kids off the streets of Harlem and keep them productive by getting them to do sports. This was a great thing for my brother and I. We did absolutely everything—mainly basketball, swimming, and ice hockey. We loved these things. I played on a basketball team in 4th and 5th grade and was pretty good! I actually met Mayor Dinkins one day; he gave me an autograph and signed it "You are the future."

Then there was a really bad day which I'll never forget for the rest of my life. The day started when our parents took us downtown to Conway to shop around. We had bought sneakers for my brother and I that were only $20. Well, I don't know what happened, but while we were at the Conway store, somehow my mother lost the bags with our sneakers. My father wasn't happy about it. He blamed us for distracting her. He was pissed the whole way home, and we were scared. When we finally got home, my father took off his belt, threw my brother and I into the bathtub and turned on the shower, where the cold water soaked our clothes. Then he began to whip us with his leather belt. I'll never forget the screaming, the sounds of the lashing of the leather belt, and my brother and I crying from all the pain. My father didn't stop there; he went on to beat my mom. This was the ONLY time I've ever seen him hit my mom and it was because she tried to stop him from beating us. To this day I get nightmares from this from which I wake up in cold sweats, and sometimes I suffer from flashbacks of the painful memories.

One night, I was sleep walking. I went into the bathroom and into the bathtub and began taking a shower with all my clothes still on! My mother I me like that she woke me from my slumber.

Living in Harlem wasn't easy for me as a young immigrant child who had an identity crisis—as I've said, I never quite fit in with Latinos because I couldn't speak fluent Spanish and I looked white to them due to my Polish side, whereas few Polish people lived in Harlem.

In our tenement on 603 West 138th Street, when you opened the steel door from the corridor, the interior was beautiful, but unfortunately it smelled of piss on the stairways and had empty crack vials on the floor—this wasn't just in my building but all over the streets of Harlem. There was also a crackhead from Puerto Rico named Flaka. No one seemed to know her real name, but my family always felt extremely bad for her. It looked like she lived in the basement underneath the stairs, and she offered all of the neighbors blowjobs for drugs. When I was around 11 or 12, I started the 5th grade at PS75, we had Mr. Liberto, who was a new teacher who I really liked. My friends Sky and Melanie were the kids I hung out with most during recess. I had a huge crush on this girl Angie but I never could work up the nerve to talk to her. I basically couldn't talk to girls, and this became a problem.

I did end up with some best friends, Alex and Max. Alex was rich; his family had another house in the Catskill Mountains of New York. I was invited there to spend a weekend. To me, it was heaven; it was quiet, and they had a cottage that made me feel warm and welcome. For breakfast we had blueberry pancakes. They also took me to my first Yankees baseball game. Max was my best friend from school. His mother worked at City College, where my father studied, and so that's how they knew each other. At first, we had playdates where Max and I would joke about everything and just kick it. But then, I began scheming on him. I always had this sense of inferiority and I felt that he was rich and we were poor kind of thing. So, I began to sell him pictures of superheroes that I had drawn and charging him absurd amounts of money for them. I would take $30 per drawing. Pretty soon, I had a lot of cash saved up because of Max. If grown-up Max is reading this, I apologize sincerely. I stole so much of his shit like a silver coin and lots of cash. In school however, I had become the quiet smart boy, who never caused any trouble, or if I did, I never got caught. Mr. Liberto, used to take me and another kid to Barnes and Noble to buy us a book each because of our good job on our homework . Of course, at the time, I absolutely loved Goosebumps, so I usually got a Goosebumps book. Other books I enjoyed a lot were *A Cricket in Times Square*, *Charlotte's Web*, and of course, *The Trumpet of the Swan*. I also partook in drama and African dance at school, Since early on, I was in plays such as *A Charlie Brown Christmas* and performed dances to songs such as to MC Hammer's "You Can't Touch This" as well as songs by MC Lyte's "Roughneck" and Kriss Kross; remember them? I was fascinated with black culture—I wanted to be cool and hip; the first cassette that I ever bought with my mother was Salt N Pepa's "Very Necessary", at the Harlem Music Hut on 125th St. And then, of course, MC Hammer—I was a huge fan! We watched a lot of shows at home including *The Simpsons, He Man, Inspector Gadget, Johnny Quest, McGuyver, GI Joe, Gargoyles, Power Rangers, Animaniacs, Pinky and The Brain, Ren and Stimpy, Doug,* and *Ghostbusters*, but probably the most influential cartoon showing back then was *The Teenage Mutant Ninja Turtles*! I was obsessed with them. Many times my brother and I spent time at Yancy's house on 135th Street after school. We would watch cartoons or play video games. Believe it or not, Yancy's father was someone who recruited coyotes to transport illegal immigrants across the border from Mexico. He tried to get my father to do it while they were drinking once, but my father declined. They loved drinking tequila, and Yancy's father always ate the little worm at the end. I never understood how someone could do that.

Another good friend of my father's was my neighbor on the 5th floor, Mr. Carvajal. We called him "vecino" which in Spanish means, "neighbor.". He had kids, Raulito and Susie, who were friends of ours. Mr. Carvajal always had parties, and he was a huge drinker. My father often partook with him while us kids played Nintendo and then Super Nintendo in Raulito's room. Sometimes we would go with Raulito to Riverbank State Park just to kick around a soccer ball, play catch or shoot some hoops. I loved going there, especially at night, and even more so with my father—when he was in a good mood.

These were times that I'll never forget, but unfortunately there were also times when I spent my time being afraid of my father. All my life he was a mysterious figure to me, like a puzzle that I just couldn't solve. I didn't get him. What was it that he wanted for us? What was happiness for him? He was almost always miserable and extremely irritable, even though when he was happy he was so charming and popular.

One night, I'm not sure exactly how the beef had happened or why but my father came in and took out a long metal stick that he kept underneath the bed. He alarmed us by telling us not to open the door, then he went out, and he and Mr. Carvajal went down to the lobby of our building and began to fight with a few of the Dominican drug dealers. I'm not sure exactly why they were fighting, all I remember is that Carvajal got some ribs broken in the fight. I remember that night I being scared as I lay in my bed. I couldn't sleep at all; the feeling of the unknown had me anxious and afraid. After about an hour or two, he finally came back but unfortunately, he didn't tell us anything. Later on, we found out that the Dominicans wanted their revenge. I found out through my mother that the Dominican dealers on the block wanted my father dead. They were even kind enough to send a funeral wreath to our door, with a note stating that they knew where my mother worked and they knew where my brother and I attended school. This really made my mother panic. She urged him to leave Harlem or else we would be soon dead, and my father took her advice. At first, we abruptly fled to Hoboken, New Jersey, where we stayed with my aunt Lenore. We stayed there for about two weeks, then my father booked us all onto a flight to Guayaquil, Ecuador in order to escape what our family was dealing with in New York.

ECUADOR

I was only about six years old, and my brother was four when we first went to Guayaquil, Ecuador. I don't however, remember much of it except for the fact that we visited my Uncle Lucho, who had a big house in Babahoyo. Ecuador is a third world country, with even more poverty around than Harlem! That trip taught me the value of traveling. One of the things I admired about my father was the fact that, no matter how poor we were as kids, he'd always take us somewhere—Orlando, FL, Ecuador, Poland, Canada: we visited them all, and I'm thankful that he was able to give us that opportunity. Anyway, I my fondest memory of Ecuador was when we were out on the farm one day, and there was a giant toad. I stepped on it not only to squish it, but I also to see what its guts looked like. My brother was disgusted, but I was really curious. Another memory of Ecuador was when we went into a jungle I , where there were real natives with red banana peels or something similar on their heads. We went deep into the jungle, where I watched a lady cut the head off of a chicken before my parents enjoyed a delicious soup made from that chicken! I didn't like it one bit, and I refused to eat it.

I remember I playing in the jungle with another boy who was a native; we were running wild and free through the brush when we came across a giant pipe-well. As a boy I obviously had to crawl through it! It was an adventure and this giant pipe was just awesome. So, I began crawling through this pipe, I but about halfway through, there was a sharp pain on my right upper arm. It hurt like hell—a hard metal object had pierced my flesh, and I could see blood pouring out of the wound. My native friend immediately ran back with me to the house where the natives began to apply some kind of green medicine found only in the jungle, before they bandaged up my arm and I was good to go.

We finally came back to New York City, and things with the Dominicans seemed to calm down. I was in my last year, fifth grade, at PS75, I we had an afterschool program. It was fun for the most part; we played lots of sports like kickball, dodgeball and basketball as well as football. I really enjoyed being with my counselor Brad, who would draw us Marvel Superheroes. I'll never forget the pictures that he drew, my favorites were the Wolverine and the Hulk! Those were some badass drawings. My mother would always be the one to pick us up afterschool, and sometimes we would stop at the store where she would buy us some chocolate or a bagel hot with butter to eat. Other times, if we were lucky, we'd go to a comic book store on Broadway and get Marvel trading cards as well as basketball cards. I was obsessed with the Knicks, I loved John Starks and Patrick Ewing! I loved Michael Jordan, I and anyone on the Dream Team in 92'.

One day at the comic book store, I got a holographic card of the infamous Spiderman V Venom. That card was actually worth a lot, but that wasn't why I was so excited. It was the fact that I knew it was special, I and it was all mine!

I had a fair few parties in that period. My fourth grade party had been at the 95th Street and Riverside Dr dinosaur park, but the most memorable one for me was when my mother celebrated my 5th grade birthday at Familia Pizzeria on 110th and Broadway. I remember I had my best friends Max, Wally, and Miguel and we got to make our own pizzas, spinning our own dough, and putting the sauce and cheese on it—a lot of fun for a kid! However, at home, I felt like I was walking on eggshells. I got pressured a lot by both my parents. My father would yell at me if I couldn't understand a math problem; he'd lock me in a room to study for hours, and even then I didn't understand math! Whenever he tried to teach me math so I could do my homework, he would berate and insult me, screaming that I was a worthless idiot, to the point where I began to cry.

Meanwhile, they were calling me "gifted" at elementary school, so my mother enrolled me to the Delta Program for the gifted. I was supposed to go to a middle school in New York City I for it. I remember when I was preparing for the tests for admission, my mother would make me cry by saying things like "If you don't get into this school you'll never be anything!" They put a lot of pressure on me as a kid. My mother was there for me in some ways but in others she wasn't. I liked it when she let me pick out a few books from the Scholastic Kids catalogue (I loved books) but hated the fact that she never stood up for me and was so submissive to my father's needs and wishes. I hated that she didn't do more to prevent the abuse from happening, instead sweeping it under the rug. I hated that she kept it secret, and most of all, I hated that the way she always would deny that he abused us and stood up for him.

There's no place in the world like New York City! You can try to replicate it but this is the city that's got its own heartbeat. And it wasn't always bad growing up with my father. One day, we entered the 5 Boroughs Bike Race. The crazy thing was, that none of my family had have expensive bikes like other bikers and yet we still competed in the race. Pablo and I just had these Huffy street bikes with green wheels and handle bars. So we rode through tunnels, bridges and through city streets, eventually completing the ride. I remember going through that last tunnel; I had to stand up from my seat to pedal, and I had almost given up as the strong wind was making my back cramp up severely. But I didn't stop, and eventually made it to the finish line. It didn't even take that long either. I was so proud of myself for doing this, and other people were giving us high fives and acknowledging how awesome it was for us to have completed the race with such crappy bikes.

My father loved biking. He'd take us down to Riverside Park and we'd ride all through it until we got to Central Park downtown and then back up again. It was a beautiful thing. I loved the parks in NYC. But one time, my father, Pablo and I had stopped in Riverside Park, in the middle of the road to drink some water. These kids from uptown started racing their bikes towards us and clearly weren't stopping. My father instantly panicked and grabbed my brother, but he didn't get me, he just yelled for me to move out of the way. But I froze like a deer in headlights as I faced the gang of 10 bikers head in the middle of the road. Well, they didn't stop, and thought they could go right through me. And I swear to god when they ran into me it didn't leave a scratch on me—their bikes just flipped and they fell down to the ground. When they got up, they said "I'm sorry man are you okay?" I said I was, and they apologized to me. But I knew right there and then that God was real. He had shielded me and provided protection. As I've indicated, my father had good moments when he really seemed to love us and care for us —when I was six or so my father took us to the City College of New York where he had studied Chemical Engineering. We went there a lot, to just take walks. He had been the one who taught me to ride my first Huffy bike. I had got on the bike and begun to pedal while he balanced me on the seat. He had run next to me while I pedaled and, before I knew it, he had let go I and I continued cycling on my own—at least I did until I realized he had let go, then I panicked and crashed the bike!

Another time my father took me to my first movie theater Sony on Broadway and 69th.I was super excited; my choice was either *Gremlins* or the *Teenage Mutant Ninja Turtles*. Of course you know that I picked the latter! I also remembered when he bought us the VHS of The Little Mermaid. He also took me to my first amusement park at 6 Flags Great Adventure. I loved spending time with my father and have some fond memories of him. There were times when he was good to me, and I did love him—but I despised him for what he did to us, so it was a complex relationship..

Another great memory comes from when our family was walking down Central Park at night and we saw Rick Moranis, who was in *Honey, I Shrunk the Kids,* playing ice hockey with his son. My father chatted to I him, and he was so down to earth.

MOVING

In August of 1995, my father had accepted a fellowship there for a Masters in Environmental Engineering at the University of Colorado at Boulder. When we were moving, it brought out the controlling aspect of my father; he would be shouting his commands and we had to adhere to them. What I remember most about moving from Harlem to Boulder was that my father threw out all of my precious books, and that completely crushed me! Not only that, but he also took the money that I had been saving up all of my childhood to buy my plane ticket. It hurt and I was deeply resentful that I couldn't express how I felt without getting my ass beat. So, why did I also resent my mother? Because she knew how I felt or what I wanted and yet she always hid my emotions and wants from my father as she didn't want to make him angry. No doubt, my mother was afraid of my father, and I knew it from a young age. Anyway, that day when we were packing, my father had kicked me out, (it wasn't the first time) and I had left in tears crying as I ran to Riverbank state park, which was my second home. I stared out into the Hudson River, knowing that I'd soon be leaving Harlem for Boulder, a place that was beautiful but in which would be a complete culture shock.

It was around 5 am and the sun had just begun to shine when Our family packed whatever few belongings we had and waited outside our building for our taxi. Our vecino was waiting for us outside on the stoop, to say goodbye. This move, which happened when I was 12 years old, would forever change my life, in a positive way.

BOULDER

Boulder was a beautiful place, probably the most beautiful place I had ever seen! It had a small mountain town feel with many college students living there. It was known for its hippies and rocket scientists, who dressed humbly, usually in t-shirts and sandals. I didn't find this out until later, but my new classmate Alexis's father was head NBA coach of the Phoenix Suns at one point! How cool is that? Anyway, we moved into university housing, where I spent some of the best years of my life.

When we first had arrived at Newton Court on Arapahoe Ave, we lived in building 2P. It was absolutely beautiful: it had a laundry room, playground, and basketball court, but most important of all was the amazing field that it had. I'll never forget that field. It's where we played all of our sports. I met tons of people who liked to play sports. In fact, as soon as we got there, I played lots of sports before I'd even started the 6th grade at Baseline Middle School.

The first friends I made were Cachee, Amber, Blake, Ryan Walters, and pretty soon I would meet AJ, who would be a great inspiration to me. AJ was the epitome of cool. He was the image of what I wanted to be—smooth and cool, but most importantly, he was amazing in EVERY sport that he played. Ryan Walters was also amazing—in fact, he would end up being an actual CU Buffs football player later, and later some kind of assistant coach in the NFL, which was awesome! Boulder carried a kind of magic that I'd never seen or felt before. We'd hang out play football until late evening, when our parents would call us to go home.

My father had bought four bikes for our family, but they were straight up embarrassing—old ass bikes that my brother and I would ride around. Although, eventually, my father bought us great mountain bikes; mine was a Trek.

Before I knew it 6th grade had started at Baseline Middle School, where I met my best friend, Devin Doyle. Devin's parents were wealthy architects. He lived up on Rose Hill Drive I ; when I first went to his house I was shocked. They had windows that covered the whole wall and beautiful paintings, and it was right on a creek, It was absolutely stunning! His parents were very welcoming, too. The first time I visited his home was when we had a project from Mr. Momberger in the 6th grade. It was an art project that we had to do, to recreate Tenochtitlan, the capital city of the Aztec empire. So it was me Consuelo, another girl in our class, and Devin, and we all met up at Devin's house to work on it. I wanted what Devin had: the beautiful house on the creek, all of it.

The locker next to mine at Baseline belonged to Natalie Mock, who was absolutely gorgeous; I had a big crush on her and also on a girl called Lauren Goodman.

I would walk home or bike from school with my Korean friend Hyung Hoon or my Saudi Arabian friend Omar. Omar, Hyung Hoon and I would all play basketball down in Newton Court. I remember one time when my parents weren't home and me and Hyung Hoon went to see the horror movie *Scream*. I 'll never forget how much that movie scared me as a twelve-year-old boy. It finished around 10pm, and I cycled back home as fast as I could! Another

I of my friends was Dan. We made a Nutri-Grain bar commercial for science class together. Later on in life, many of my friends would become doctors, including Dan, Omar as well as Wumesh.

Another great thing about Boulder was riding trails over the mountains. My favorite was Boulder Creek, where I often biked and rollerbladed. I also fell in love with the Boulder Public Library, which like no other library that I had ever seen. It had an espresso cafe, from which I would get chocolate-covered coffee beans. I'd also meet Devin here, and do reports for extra credit. I spent a lot of time at the library, reading and checking out books. I remember one night the library was closing at 9pm; my father had yelled at me and kicked me out of the house to make sure I returned a few overdue books. I remember that night it was almost closing time and I was racing through the Boulder Creek path alone. I saw this pack of raccoons which scared the bejesus out of me! I finally returned the books. So much of how I behaved or what I reacted to was because of my father rushing me or yelling at me; later on in life I would develop a sense of urgency in everything I did.

It was clear, however, that we were different from other people. Maybe it wasn't as evident because we lived in family housing with other minorities who shared similar lifestyles as us, but to the Americans, we were different. For example, after a football game my friend Mark had us over at his home for a party. His house was so huge, it had a fucking elevator in it! He'd tell people that his grandfather invented radio waves or something like that.

I Sometimes I wanted money for the movies or for TCBY ice cream, and my mother didn't have it. I feel bad that I was an asshole and I demanded it, because I was so tired of having nothing. We loved TCBY; as a family we would go there occasionally where my mother, being Polish, would order the white chocolate "mouse" (mousse). I became a self-starter, an entrepreneur at an early age. I was offering babysitting services at 12 years old, and also had a paper route, which when my family sometimes helped me with when they were bored. I loved money, probably because we grew up not having much of it.

Around this time I met Wumesh and Bhusan; they were brothers who lived living in Marine Court, the next apartments over to where I lived. They were the ones who first introduced me to street hockey; I remember my parents buying me my first pair of rollerblades. They were Bauer hockey rollerblades, size 12, and I'll never forget them. With my blades and my hockey stick I would meet up with a bunch of those kids in Marine Court to play street hockey. I was actually really good at it from my days of ice skating in Riverbank State Park. I knew how to shoot great goals and how to hockey stop, so I was pretty much awesome. There was this kid Wicke, who was always on the other team to me; he was bigger and taller than me as well as older. When we played football, I was quarterback and it was always me against him. One time I threw the ball and hit him in the face; he was quite badly hurt, but accepted it and we moved on. Nothing made me feel as good as playing sports, man, it felt phenomenal!

Living in Newton Court in Boulder got me very close to the Buffs players. I remember we met one first-year player who happened to live in Newton Court. We'd visit him and we would party with him and his girlfriend at the time. The coolest thing about this Buffs player was that he would let us into the CU Buffaloes training facilities, even eventually giving us the code to get in! So my brother and I would access their training room and steal everything we could get our hands on. We'd steal autographed gloves, and footballs signed by Rashaam Salaam and other famous players whom added value to it. Years later I felt sorry for what I had done. I must've stolen thousands of dollars worth of shit, but at the time, we were just two kids that went gaga for the CU Buffs. We were just kids, and we didn't know any better.

In the summer of 7th grade my father sent me to Kids Kamp. Most of the staff were very cool—they were college students. I met Luis, a Mexican teen, there; he would sing the rap lyrics to NWA's "Fuck the Police". He didn't like white people, and tried to teach us about "brown power." We were rebellious at 13, and wanted the whole world to know it. Anyway, one day, we skipped camp and went to a soccer store in Boulder; it was me Luis, Mason and this kid Collin. Collin distracted the owner of the store while me, Luis, Mason and I began stealing Adidas wallets. I still have it to this day. The owner caught us, and we were in big trouble. She contacted Kids Kamp and we were suspended from going on a field trip to Fun Plex. Just for once, my father didn't say much about it, which was a surprise.

Another time, a kid who lived in Newton Court started a fight with me on the basketball court. I don't know what had gotten into me but I punched him in the face and cracked his glasses, which fell on the floor. Well, he had an older bigger brother, who he ran off to fetch. I ran really fast to my house in a panic and began crying to my father telling him what I had done. Again, he didn't say much, in fact he wasn't even mad. It was always difficult to predict how he would react to a situation.

I'll never forget a biking accident I had in Boulder. I'd often ride my bike fast, without using the brakes, down Folsom Hill. I was probably 13 at the time, and as I was going down the hill this way, there were these two guys walking. Being the smart ass that I was tried to just swerve around them, but it didn't work. The terrain was uneven and my bike flipped so that I fell hard onto the ground, head first. The two guys immediately ran over to me asking if I was alright and offering to call an ambulance. I was hurt pretty badly; I had bumped by head, and scraped the shit out of my right arm, elbow, and my right leg. There was blood everywhere—but even with all that, I said no to them calling the ambulance because I was so afraid of how my father would react. I limped home to Newton Court, where I passed out. I remember that I had gauze wrapped all around my arm and leg from going to get myself checked out, but my father didn't like it so he made me take it off and let the wounds heal fresh.

Even with all of the friends and people I associated with in Boulder, deep down I felt like I didn't really have a sense of belonging. Sure, I played sports but there were times in the summers when I would get depressed; my mother would just say "don't be depressed" while my father's way of dealing with things was to tell me to walk 8 miles a day. In school I would still be the shy quiet kid, but, on the football field or basketball court, if someone started something with me I'd flip out, get in a rage and fight them. That was the other thing about me, I couldn't control my emotions.

During our time in Boulder, my father signed both me and my brother up for Judo classes at the YMCA. We worked out three times a week, and I earned a yellow belt.

When I was 13, my father graduated in his Masters of Environmental Engineering; it was a big day for him. Soon he began to work (finally) for the Boulder Conservation testing the acidity of waters and lakes, and shit like that. We ended up moving to another apartment since we couldn't live at the family housing anymore. I really liked our new place; it was a townhouse with carpet and it was two stories high. This was where I met Manny, a Mexican who was the same age as me. Manny was trouble, but he had one thing that I wanted: girls. We used to go to Crossroads Mall and get cologne samples, and sometimes my brother would come as well. One day, I lost Manny at the mall. I went outside to get my bike only to find that Manny was deflating my bike's tires! When I confronted him, he said that he was only doing it as a joke. I began to distance myself from him after that. Manny and a friend would fuck girls right outside my window so I could see. My father would just close the blinds. But he was definitely something else.

In 8th grade at Baseline Middle School, for history day I went as Colin Powell, because of what he represented; he was from Harlem and all that. I was so nervous I was panicking but eventually I got into my costume and all was well. Another time for 8th grade, the teacher wanted us to talk about our "immigrant story" but I realized that I was terrified of public speaking, and so I didn't do it. She let me write my experience as an essay, but I always hated the fact that I couldn't do it.

I also played basketball for the team, but I was second string. I was the kid who got yelled at and took a lot of abuse from my coach because I was always messing up drills and plays. Him yelling like that was uncalled for and didn't help solve the problem. I have a strong opinion on coaching in youth sports—this is done for the benefit of the kids, and no kid should have a coach who is too aggressive with them or takes the game too seriously. He would yell at me, call me names and embarrassing me, and, at that time, I didn't know that that wasn't okay. It wasn't my fault. Along with my anxiety I had problems paying attention and following directions, and that's why I didn't do well on team sports. There was, however, one game that we played where I was great at. After hearing "Mo Money Mo Problems", I got so excited that I started playing ball like a pro, one time shooting and scoring 8 points in the first quarter. The coach was so impressed with me that he gave a heartfelt speech about me being the MVP of that game after it ended.

There was a girl I liked called Lilly, who actually went on a date with me in 7th grade or 8th grade. When we talked on the phone, my anxiety was so bad that I could barely even speak to her! When we finally met, we went ice skating. It was a terrible date because I barely spoke to her the whole time and my mother came along as well. Later, in class, she wrote me a note that basically said, "Talk to the people you like. Get to know them." I never forgot that, because it was so hard to do, especially with girls.

I was enjoyed choir, and not to toot my own horn, but I was really good. I was a bass, and Ms. Rollins, who was our choir teacher often let me do jazz solos. We sang so many great songs. I especially liked the jazz quartet we had. We sang great songs such as "I Only Have Eyes For You", "Lullaby of Birdland", and other classics. I also loved hip hop; for drama class, I remember we put on black sunglasses and sang Coolio's "Gangsta's Paradise". I bought my first CD in Boulder: Biggie's *Life After Death*, I loved Puff Daddy and Biggie and all of Bad Boy and 2pac and the West side. There was a CD store in the mall; every night I would go with my brother and we could listen to any CD we wanted to. I cannot tell you how many times I listened to "I'll Be Missing You" and "Can't Nobody Hold Me Down."

On the last day at middle school, there was a tornado in the area and we all had to stay in the basement of the school. I said my last goodbyes to all my friends, then rode my bike home as fast as I could because I was worried about the tornado. Summer came, and many of my friends who lived in Newton Court like AJ moved away to Texas. I was a rebellious young man who seemed to get into trouble a lot, even though I wasn't really a trouble maker! I just wanted nothing more than to fit in; I remember hanging out with Zak Kiernan, who had been one of my close friends since we made that rap video in middle school. I would spend nights at Zak's house, and we'd smoke and walk over to the Hill, where he took me to my first techno club, at which I felt very awkward. I was also friends with Aspen, David, Forest, and Anthony. Aspen pitched in and she got me a beeper for my 14th birthday. That summer after middle school, I got my first "official" job for the Boulder Youth Corps. This was not an easy job at all; in fact it was probably one of the hardest jobs I've ever had. Our job was to maintain the trails of Boulder; we had to carry shovels and other tools like that, and work in the sun. It definitely wasn't easy! I wanted to quit so many times, but my mother made me stay until summer was over.

    I remember my first week of Boulder High School.. I was extremely shy and nervous throughout this first week because there were cliques everywhere and I didn't know where I fit in. For lunch they had an open concept style; people would go out to nearby fast food places. The best thing about the school for me was their music madrigals program—I tried out and became only the second freshman ever to make Madrigals in the school's history! That great feeling wouldn't last however, as a week later my father told us that he had got a job for the Environmental Protection Agency and we were going to move to Boston, MA.

NORWOOD 98-02'

We first arrived in Norwood in the fall of 1998, a week before high school started for me. It was a suburb 18 miles south of Boston. Our family moved into a two-bedroom apartment in an apartment complex called Windsor Gardens. I was severely depressed because I had left all of my friends, especially Devin, in Boulder. My father didn't seem to care how I felt. The fact that I had been happy in Boulder didn't matter to him. He just made us pack our shit and, just like that, we were in Norwood, MA.

For my first year as a Freshman at Norwood High School, Mr. Grazado was my guidance counselor who he helped me pick out my classes. I remember going to my first class, Earth Science, where I was sitting in the front of the classroom. I took against the teacher because he was the type of teacher that taught for 15 minutes and left the other 45 minutes for our class to socialize and shoot the shit and do whatever. So while everyone got into groups and talked I was the only one sitting in my seat not knowing what to do with myself. I felt extreme anxiety; sometimes classmates called me over to join them but I went up, got bored or was too anxious so I sat down in my seat again. Other times girls would come up to me just because they felt sorry for me. They tried to include me in their groups, but I just couldn't do it at the time. Those feelings of nervousness, inferiority and shame and fear all mixed within me; to this day I'll never forget the intensity of those feelings.

At the time I blamed my parents because all of this anxiety could have been easily avoided with medication. My parents knew that my maternal grandmother had been schizophrenic. I resented my parents for even having decided to have children together knowing that the mental illness genes could easily be passed down to my brother or I. Around this time was where the problems socially and bullying began. But I did eventually meet a group of best friends that I'd go on adventures with. So for me Norwood High School was the best of times and the worst of times—a gift and a curse.

I joined the Freshman Choir. The central theme of high school was my social anxiety; sometimes the music teacher made me sing out loud and I couldn't do it in front of the class, so I had to turn my back away from the rest of my classmates! Because of the social anxiety I got bullied and teased a lot, especially when I took up Latin in sophomore year (but more on that later).

My first year in Norwood was tough, but it had some good times. I joined the freshman football team as a defensive tackle, and everyone on the team was awesome: people like Manny Lopes, Ryan Trus, Pat Foley, Sean Murphy, and others. They were good to me and I'll never forget their kindness. They all welcomed me to their town, Norwood, which is in the Guinness Book of World Records as having the most citizens who remain there, raise families there and never leave.

One day we were on the bus coming back from winning a game when the guys started shouting "Party at Jan's House!" Manny asked me if that'd be okay, I said sure! You have to understand that I had just moved to Norwood, and I wanted more than anything to fit in and be cool. But the party later on that night was a complete disaster for me. They all came over to Windsor Gardens to our apartment, where everyone sat in silence. Almost the whole team was there. It was very awkward, especially for me. My mother cut up some strawberries for everyone to eat, but it didn't really go well. After a while, everyone left my house, and later on in school some other classmates would gossip about how they went to Jan's house to party, and the apartment had no furniture! I was embarrassed; my father had just began to make money at his first job, working as an environmental engineer for the EPA. So my point is that my father was finally making a decent salary, but he was frugal when it came to spending money, not only on furniture, but on my brother and I. We still had hand me down clothes, or clothes that were years old. But the worst part of it all was the fact that I felt inferior to all the other Irish and Italian kids at my school. Norwood High consisted of predominantly white kids, and I hated the fact that they all seemed to not be struggling financially. They had nice clothes, many of them began driving towards the end of freshman year, and they all came from houses that their parents owned. They were settled and nested in the comfort of the American Dream—that feeling of being settled is something I never had, which made me hungry and ambitious.

That was one thing that really bothered me about my parents. When I asked my mother when we would be buying a house she would say things like "your friends who have houses were born here and their houses were bought 30 years ago when the housing market was cheap. It didn't matter to me though, because I saw a disproportionate inequality between our financial lifestyle and those of my peers.

I went to a few more football parties, I remember this kid from Xaverian High School shaved my head at one of them. Again, I was young and dumb, and would do anything just to fit in.

In freshman choir we would have concerts or travel to districts, where we would compete over who had the best voice. I remember one time we traveled on a bus; our choir along with the sophomore choir stopped by Bickford's in Walpole, and of course everyone was ordering nice meals, and I couldn't afford it. Why? Because my mother only gave me 50 cents, which was enough for a bagel with butter. As I reflect on these memories, a lot of my shame comes from these types of experiences, when all I could afford at that restaurant was a bagel with butter, while everyone enjoyed plenty of food. When we had concerts at the Junior High South it also bothered me that my parents were never there because they either were working or they just didn't care. So I'd often have to walk to the concerts, then beg people for rides home. Football was the same; it was actually one of the reasons why I quit, even though that freshman year we had had an undefeated season. It was also because I had broken my middle finger on my right hand and couldn't participate in the game. (Which also meant I couldn't use that one for traffic anymore). After football practice and games, all the parents were there to pick up their sons from football. I was the only one whose father, who had finally bought a 1998 Toyota Camry, never showed up to pick me up. Sometimes friends would offer me rides, but they would get mad if I continually asked them for rides home and say, "Doesn't your family have a car?" I remember Dan Reen, captain of the JV Team, would occasionally give me rides after practice. Dan was a true leader; he was one of the original Norwood kids who welcomed me into the community, especially the football community. I guess he felt bad watching me walk home holding my football pads and gear. It was the saddest thing in the world to me to walk home after a concert or a football game alone in the dark, without my parents there to support and cheer me on.

Years later Dan would be killed in a car accident. He was a good guy, a true one-of-a-kind guy.

For choir we'd go to districts competitions, where I often got the highest score out of all my classmates. You know that I was the second freshman to get into madrigals in the history of Boulder High! So when the music teacher at the new school auditioned me for madrigals, I was shocked to find out that I had made alternate! I made fucking backup? Are you kidding me?! She told me that I had made alternate but if anyone dropped out then I'd be in. I was really angry so, when she wanted me in the following year's Concert Chorale as a sophomore, , I dropped out. She was upset, but it upset me more that I wasn't good enough for *her* madrigals. If you ask me, she was playing favorites. Back at home my father would tell me things like, "Why are you in a choir, are you going to pursue a career in music? That's stupid. It doesn't make any sense!" This also influenced me to drop out.

Windsor Gardens was at first a scary place, because I didn't know anyone. One of the first friends I did meet was George. He was a loner just like me who had a troubled past and lived with both parents also in my apartment complex. We would find people to buy us a 30 rack of Budweiser beer, and we'd drink in the woods. It was around age 15 when I had first began drinking beer with George. I did it to fit in; I thought that the more that I could drink the more of a "man" I was, boy was I wrong.

There was something really odd and off about drinking alone in the woods at night; it just didn't seem right. George was fucking weird. He was quiet when he drank; so much so that I took off on him one night, and went back to my house, because I felt wrong just sitting in the woods drinking. He chased me, and eventually we made up. But I still went home. Another time, I got New England

Patriot J'juan Cherry to buy us beer. It was me and another one of my first friends, Demetrious , who I had met in freshman year in choir and football named Demetrious. I actually became friends with J'juan, he was a nice guy, and I was star struck of course because he was an NFL player. I remember Demetrious and I went to J'Juan's house, and J'juan let me drive his Escalade at 14 years old to the liquor store! I remember the exact hip hop song that was playing at the time, Lil Wayne's "Tha Block is Hot"! You see, Windsor Gardens was home to a few Patriots football players, including Kevin Faulk and Michael Bishop. But my fondest memories are of my friendship with J'juan Cherry-. He was a cool guy who loved women and partying.

My brother Pablo, seemed to be making friends pretty easily. We met some Russians who we got along with great; we all looked out for one another.

My brother would either hang out or go BMX biking with them. I'd occasionally go along; they would do "jumps" with their BMX bikes and I'd do it with my mountain bike. I played lots of basketball too. In my first year at Norwood High I met Aleksey at the Civic Center. I was there almost every weekend playing ball. Aleksey was from Belarus, which used to be part of Poland. He became one of my best friends throughout high school. He lived in Windsor Gardens, but later his family moved to a small condo in Stoughton, another suburb of Boston. In Windsor Gardens I became friends with all of the Russians, including Yuri, his sister Zoya, Sergei, Mikaylo and Constantine, who were brothers, and others. We spent hours playing basketball and it started to feel like I was part of a community again, just like in Boulder.

But back home it wasn't a good situation for either me or my brother Pablo. My father was stressed out from work and he didn't like us not following his strict rules. He would beat my brother and I for silly things such as not listening to what he was saying. All throughout high school, the intensity of his beatings became worse and worse, so I tried to get help. I remember telling my guidance counselor at Norwood High about my father and being physically abused, and he just replied with, "your father just loves you and cares about you," as he smiled at me. This was wrong. I knew it was wrong: A guidance counselor is a mandated reporter and it was his responsibility to report this as abuse to the proper authorities which he never did. My father berated me and was extremely hard on me; for instance, he called me a "fucking animal." I can understand a few things that maybe contributed to his anger—stress from his government job at the EPA, the fact I had received unconditional love from my mother, which he never got, and the fact that he thought I was "mentally ill" and unfit to be a productive member of society. To be honest, I hid his abuse from everyone until about sophomore year, when I couldn't hold it in any longer. I was socially awkward, and I was wearing clothes that were years old. In my freshman year my mother had convinced my father to buy me a pair of Tommy Hilfiger jeans. So I got a pair at the Wrentham Outlets, and my father could never just shut up about the price: $45 (they were on sale) I had begun working at my first job in Norwood, at a clothing store called Decelle near my house. But I had anxiety attacks at the register- the panic attacks were so bad that I couldn't function and would even give out the wrong change! They had me greeting customers when they entered the store, and folding clothes instead of being a cashier.

Another, much better job was working as a telemarketer at a home improvement company. I invented the name "Dick Johnson" and became really good at setting appointments for the company.

The company profited well by hiring high school kids to do their appointments for them, paying them a mere $5, per appointment set. It was total bullshit, and I worked there for a while, probably around two years. Yet again, my parents never picked me up and so I either had to walk home from there or I'd get a ride, sometimes from the boss, Bob. I met a lot of cool people working that job, and eventually I even worked at a trade show, marketing the company's products at the Bayside Expo Center. I was great at sales/marketing but eventually I got fired from that company for socializing too much, and not really caring about setting appointments anymore.

My depression continued throughout freshman year and my parents took me to see a psychologist. He was an older man who took his job too seriously; my father told him how I had quit the football team, and the psychologist asked me if this was true and why I had quit. He asked me whether, if my father hadn't told him if I would have told him that. I confirmed that I would have told him, but that the reason for me quitting was that I had broken my finger during practice. But honestly, I mainly just laughed at the idea of seeing a psychologist at 15. I just didn't understand the point of it and that I needed help, even though I really did. Anyway, the psychologist told my parents that he couldn't force me to see him if I didn't want therapy, which at that age, I didn't.

That summer of 1999, before sophomore year, my father wanted me to keep busy, so he enrolled me in cowboy camp, somewhere in Colorado. It wasn't really cowboy camp, I just call it that because the majority of people there were racist cowboys from my point of view.

This was the first time I really experienced racism. I completely didn't fit in; I remember a couple of the guys trying to pick a fight with me because I accidentally stepped on a girl's toe. I was called a "spic"—at the time I didn't even know what the word meant! I isolated and I didn't even try to adapt to other people there. I didn't get along with them nor fit in, and I could care less. One kid told me I didn't have any friends there, and that hurt. But it was the truth. I didn't belong. These were sons and daughters of farmers in Colorado. I couldn't care less about the issues that they faced in their communities when it couldn't relate to me. I couldn't wait to get home. That was just two weeks of hell.

SOPHOMORE YEAR

Sophomore year was probably my toughest year. This was the year when I had met Jose, another Hispanic boy. He had a few younger brothers and lived in an apartment complex just like me. Because of this and the fact there weren't many minorities at Norwood High, I felt like Jose and I had a lot in common. I met him in biology class; in fact, he had started out bullying me. He teased me, especially because I liked the Backstreet Boys, and so of course the rest of the guys in biology class teased me as well. They did it because they knew that I would blush and get easily embarrassed. The funny thing is that Jose and I ended up becoming one of my best friends, and introduced me to other people I got along with, mainly players from the soccer team.

I ended up being friends with a group of six guys because of Jose and George. It was Jose, me, an Italian guy named Giuseppe, George, Ming, a Chinese smart ass who had just transferred from another state, and Jun, a timid funny Korean kid who we had given a nickname of Bok Choi. We all gave each other nicknames. I was "Yanni Bear," Giuseppe was "old man" or "G Spot," George was "Pilgrim" and Jose was "Nelly bear." There was also a friend that I recruited into our group named Matt. Matt already had a nickname, which was "Spunge," because of his last name. He was an awesome kid; I met him in class and we instantly became best friends. Spunge was a total band geek when I met him. He had very few friends, before he started hanging out with us. He also became my best friend in high school. He was funny, humble, and loyal.

We began sitting at lunch together; it felt good to have our own little clique going on. Giuseppe was a know-it-all from Norwood; He was an Italian kid who called me and Jose "spics" and Ming a "chink." We all assumed that he was just playing around, but in retrospect I wonder if that was true. Giuseppe had a man cave at his house and was one of the first people who got his driver's license, so he could drive us around in his black Pontiac Grand Prix. The man cave in his basement was one of our first hangout spots; it was the first place I officially got drunk; when my parents picked me up my mother immediately said she could smell the beer on me. They knew I was drunk; of course they did. But it wasn't ultra drunk like I'd get later on in life, it was just a few beers.

I wasn't happy at home. My father would still beat me for every single thing with his leather belt. I took a lot of it out on my brother Pablo. I remember hitting him in the face with a Timberland shoe once; even worse was the time when I hit him in the arm with a tennis racket so hard that we both worried that I broke his arm. I remember the Norwood Police coming up to our house to check on us. My father wanted to call the police every time I bothered my brother; he said I was abusive, can you believe that shit? Anyway, when the police came, they took my brother to our neighbors in Windsor Gardens, who were from India and knew our family pretty well. Our family had to go to court because of this, and the judge kept asking "do you have a speech impediment young man?" I'll never forget those words. Because honestly, I was nervous as shit being in court facing a judge. But the case was dismissed.

The judge, however, gave my father the contact for someone in power in the district court system. I'm not sure if she was a prosecutor or someone else, but we went to pay her a visit and she basically told me that I was nothing but a criminal, and that if things didn't change, I'd end up in jail. I was horrified, even though I knew this wasn't me. I guess her plan was to help motivate me to change me for the better; but of course she didn't know about what my father had been doing to me and my brother all these years.

LATIN CLASS AT NORWOOD HIGH

Another bad experience was Latin class. This probably hit me hardest because of all the teasing. You see, after I dropped out of concert chorale, I needed to find another class so I figured I'd pick up Latin. Demetrius, my friend from football and music, was the one who encouraged me to take up Latin. He said it was a fun class and that I'd enjoy it. I'm sorry that I believed him, because he was setting me up. Everyone in that class made fun of me—especially my hair. Even my so called "friend" Demetrius made fun of me, and so did my other "friend" Dave. You see the problem was that my family never took me to get haircuts. I only went every three or four months, so my hair looked terrible—they nicknamed me "Puffy" because of this. They would rank on me simply because they knew that I reacted nervously and blushed easily; worst of all, our teacher, didn't do shit to stop it. One day, my friend TJ, who knew about my situation at home, literally gave me the shirt off his back (more on that later) and I was wearing this awesome bright orange PNB shirt that he had given me. Well the kids in Latin didn't like it, especially one of my classmates, who asked where I had got it. They were teasing me and busting my balls because of it. The class had older classmen that were a year or two older than me as well, but it didn't stop them from talking shit about me.

Another bully was Jack. He was a nothing who picked on me because I was vulnerable and sensitive. One day at the bus stop I was wearing a North Face jacket that was three times my size! (As I said before, my parents were bargain hunters and very frugal when it came to buying my brother and I clothes—so they had given me this jacket that was way too big for me and I looked like a clown in it). This made me a prime target for bullies. Jack was throwing pencils at me from the back of the bus. I felt like an idiot as I just turned around and weakly said, "who was that?". I hated myself for the fact that I couldn't stand up for myself. When he saw me in the halls he'd push me into the lockers and I didn't do shit about it.

Before Jose, Spunge and I became best friends. Jose had been teasing me and making fun of me in biology class. Given everything that was going on at home and at school I had to take out my aggression somewhere-and that somewhere was in gym—when we played handball. I LOVED the sport; it was similar to something like lacrosse where you'd run with a ball and could check people and score. I was the KING of handball! Ask about me! Everything that was going on at home I'd take out on the court; it was awesome! I was a beast! Anyway, it'd always end up being me versus another great football player who was also a big guy—Pat Foley. He'd go after me to try and stop me from scoring goals and I'd go after him for the same thing. There was a girl in our grade who was also in my gym class—Elisa, who was from Spain.

I thought she was the finest girl I'd ever seen. She talked to me because of my handball skills; my one regret was that I didn't talk to her more in high school-because she was gorgeous!

One day, I really took my aggression out through handball. The night before my father had tried to pull me off my bed by my hair and I couldn't take it anymore. I took his hand off my hair and stood up yelling "Don't fucking touch me! Don't fucking touch me!" Well, I've always heard that when you stand up to bullies, they get scared and that's what happened with my father. He ran to the living room where he picked up the stick that kept the balcony closed and walked toward our room. He was clearly going to beat me with the stick, and when I saw him angrily approaching us I pushed the door to keep him out and yelled out to my brother Pablo to call the police. Pablo began crying and didn't know what to do. Eventually, my father left us alone, but I was still filled with anger and rage. So, the next day I had a lot of anger to release, and I took it out on Jose. Given that Jose kept making fun of me in biology class I was shocked when he claimed to be my friend. After the handball that day, when we were in the locker room, I went off on him. I started shouting at him to leave me the fuck alone. I even punched the lockers and he was scared stiff. You see, it's funny how people bother you and pick on you until you lose your shit, and when you lose your shit, you're the problem and they suddenly become the victim, not you. Anyway, I was going off on him when Pat Foley saw me, and he intervened. He tried to separate us and then began to calm me down. I had had it with getting teased by someone who was supposedly "my friend." He was no friend of mine if he was teasing me and this had to stop. After that, believe it or not, our relationship grew stronger; Jose had my back more than ever before, and never again did he tease me in biology class.

These were the types of problems that I was having at school. You see, people who insulted or teased me or were against me at school never realized that the reason I was so weak and a target of bullying because of what was happening at home.

I remember another time when I needed a cell phone. I was about 16 years old and I saved up and got a Nokia cell phone for myself. When my father picked me up at the Walpole Mall, as he was driving on Route 1 he exploded on me. He yelled at me for getting the phone; he always thought he was right about everything, and it bothered me. He told me that I didn't need a phone and that I was trying to be a pimp. He pulled over abruptly on the side of Route 1 and told me to get the fuck out and walk home. It was at least five or six miles to Windsor Gardens from Route 1, but I walked it. I hated him.

Sophomore year was probably my hardest year but I survived it and so can you. I can completely relate to anyone who is going through bullying or getting teased at school-I know it's hard and I feel for you if you are. The key is to stand up to your bully. I know it's not easy, but it's something that has to be done. Looking back, my biggest and most dangerous bully was not the kid that threw pencils, or the kids who teased me about my hair just to see my face blush—it was my own father.

Osei and TJ

In the summer right before freshman year I had met Mike Osei, a cool guy from Ghana. We instantly became friends; I'd visit his home which was in Windsor Gardens also. Our friendship was based on hip hop music—he'd burn CDs of all the new rap albums out. He also introduced me to TJ, who was a mysterious, quiet but incredibly intelligent kid who also lived in Windsor Gardens but went to Milton Academy. It was one of the most prestigious schools out there—presidents have gone there, so to get into that school you have to be pretty smart. TJ lived in Norwood but he also had a home on the Mattapan-Milton line. Sometimes we'd hang out there. TJ is essential in my story because he was the first one to take me under his wing and show me the beauty of urban culture and hip hop. He taught me to be true to my identity, while at the same time showing me that I am a Latino male, which meant should take care of my hair and the style of dress. He tried social experiments with me to see if he could dress me a certain way, like in in street/urban clothes to see if I could pass as a legitimate Hispanic male in Mattapan, his hood. He was so happy when it worked and the kids accepted me as Latino. I was accepted in Mattapan, TJ's neck of the woods! TJ was extremely intelligent and had deep conversations with me about race and life in general. He had told me that he had been shot in the foot when he was little and his family had had been kidnapped in Nigeria. He also told me that he had met the President of the United States, Bill Clinton—of course at first, I didn't believe him. One problem I had with TJ was the fact that he always was smarter than me. We'd get into arguments, and he'd check me, and I was mad that I couldn't do anything to rebut him. I had met his mother Tara, a white woman of Scottish-Irish descent as well as his older brother Geoffrey and his father, who was full blooded Nigerian, and was mentally unstable—but he was also a genius. He had invented the first personal computer in his country. TJ told me stories about him and his father clashing, and about how he was physically abused by his father as well. He'd tell me that while he would study, he'd hear his neighbor beat his girlfriend and he would sit there and listen to her crying. I told TJ about what was happening at my house with my father, and he asked what my parents did for a living. He replied, "You just have family problems." He was right, but it affected every aspect of my life.

Mike, TJ and I instantly became inseparable friends. We'd go try to pick up girls at the Dedham movie theatres, take the commuter rail to South Station and go to Downtown Crossing to look at gold chains, visit TJ's other house on the Milton-Mattapan line, where we'd order bacon and onion pizza from Dominos. Sometimes we would take the commuter rail to Ruggles where TJ took me to a black barber to cut my hair. He said that I was Hispanic and should groom myself well. He was the first one to teach me about Black and Dominican barbershops and the great job that they do cutting a man's hair. He was the one who taught me about a good lineup—we actually spoke a lot about hair during the course of our friendship! One night we were coming home on the red line to the Milton/Mattapan trolley and there were these two white girls who we began flirting with. Well one of the girls ended up giving me her number, and told me to call her. I even made out with her. You have to understand that I was 15 at this point in my life and horny as fuck—so I definitely had plans of calling her. However, the evening took a downturn as we were leaving her house when she said bye to me and called TJ and Osei "niggers." They were so mad at this; I was just shocked but didn't immediately grasp the immensity of what this girl had just done. TJ and Osei both wanted me to tear up the piece of paper with the girl's number on it. I didn't want to at first, because obviously I wanted to date this girl and get some "play" with her. But their friendship meant more to me than the stupid racist girl. So they finally convinced me to tear up the piece of paper. Both TJ and Osei opened up to me about their experiences with racism that night—I'll be honest, it was an occasion that really opened up my eyes. It also made me wonder if people saw black people in a certain way, how did they see me? They told me that they were watched and followed every time they went into a department store, or anywhere really. I sympathized with them, and listened as they spoke angrily against the unfair treatment they received.

What I loved most about TJ was that not only was he the most intelligent person I'd ever met, but probably the best dressed person ever! I loved his style: Timberlands with jeans and a hoodie or a long tunic (long white shirt a couple of sizes too large). He wore very urban cool shit-such as a Home Depot jacket or an M&Ms jacket. One day we were talking about my clothes and I was telling him about how my family didn't provide clothing for me, and he sympathized. He had everything he wanted in terms of clothes. Well anyway, TJ said that I could have this orange PNB Nation shirt because he wanted me to dress more according to my culture. As I said, he literally took off the shirt off his back to give it to me! He was a good friend, and I'll never forget this act of kindness from him. When I wore it to school the next day in school, the other classmates looked at me funny. They just didn't understand my sense of style. As I said, the kids in Latin laughed at it and continued to make fun of it afterward. When they asked where I bought my shirt, I told them Boston.

There was no denying that TJ was a truly special person, but there was a lot of pain in him, and you could tell he was hiding something from the world. I connected with him through the music, however. One of the coolest things about his room in Windsor Gardens where he and his family lived was that it was where he used to make beats, through this program called Fruity Loops; he also rapped. He had a stand-up microphone that we used to rap and freestyle in. The kid was ridiculously talented, and I wanted to be just like him! I remember we were freestyling one day and he spit something that to this day I'll never forget! He rapped, "Niggas been spendin' Christmas rotting in jail… black tribal warriors fighting hordes of white animals now who the goriest? Yo yo yo confused ever since I was a kid." I'm telling you that rap stuck with me throughout the years and to this day I remember it, as it was that good! He also produced amazing music that was so professional, and ahead of its time. TJ also had a rap group called the Black Spadez; I was lucky enough to be featured on the debut album. We worked together and he let me write my first rap song to this slow morose beat. It took us a few hours because he was such a perfectionist and wanted my raps to be excellent. I remember writing some stupid line, it went like "dudes be gorillas they straight bananas." He did not like that line and said that we wouldn't use it in the song. I was discouraged a couple of times but inspired by him at the same time. He was my role model. I held him in such high regard. Once when

I was around 16 years old he even told me that he knew that he'd be famous one day, that it was destined to be. He was so self-assured it felt like he was predicting the future. Me and TJ were friends throughout my high school years—but towards the end of high school I went one way, and he went another. He was accepted by the prestigious Stanford University, and we pretty much lost touch for years. Eventually I found him on Facebook and sent him a message. He responded and we talked for just a bit but that level of closeness wasn't there anymore. TJ did become a famous rapper, better known to the world as Jidenna. He rose to fame with his song "Classic Man" back in 2015.

I do think about our friendship often, and it hurts me to know that he doesn't ever call or message me anymore-but at the same time I can understand that he has fame now, and probably doesn't have time to reach out to old friends. Mike Osei Mensah would pass away from surgery complications years later in February of 2018. I went to the funeral and was shocked to see my old best friend from high school in a casket, dead, and lifeless. I didn't cry though, until his little sister Denise talked about Mike—she spoke from the heart and when I saw her tear up, I began to do the same. The crazy part is that during the funeral, I didn't see TJ there. But then I saw a picture of him on Facebook as he went to the memorial the next day. It's a shame I didn't end up going to the memorial; had I gone I would've seen him.

DRIVERS ED AND FIRST CAR

During sophomore year I was excited about learning how to drive (like any other teenager) and was eager to take driving lessons from Diane. She was an older lady who was took me out driving; I remember how nervous I was when one time when there were two other girls in the car with me watching me drive. Diane kept saying "turn left here" and I was so nervous I wasn't hearing her; then the girls would tease me, saying things like "Jan do you know your left from your right?" Anyway, I also drove with my father who would berate and yell at me while practicing driving in his Toyota Camry, his precious baby. He loved that car more than he loved us. His shouting and yelling at me gave get terrible anxiety. At one point I was going to turn left on Route 1 and he yelled at me to stop the car because it was a red light. It was excruciatingly embarrassing and painful ever dealing with him; it was the same thing when he was trying to teach me math. He'd yell profanities and shame me, until I began crying and completely shut down.

Eventually I got my license, after failing it twice. Of course Demetrious told everyone in Latin class, so of course they started teasing me. Demetrious and the other kid I mentioned were two-faced. They were nice to my face but talked behind my back. That was the reality of the situation.

I had money saved up from working as a marketing specialist and savings from working at Decelle clothing store, so when I got my license I immediately went shopping for a used car. George took me to a used car dealer in Pembroke where I almost bought a Buick Regal but when I showed it to my father he didn't approve of it. He didn't want me to have a car at all but it wasn't his say. Next, I found a pearl-white 1987 Chrysler Fifth Ave that I purchased from a kid in Franklin, MA, using a check to pay him. When my father saw that I had bought it, he was livid and kicked the car! A few days later the kid who sold me the car came back with his mother; they were very upset with me. It turned out that my father had "frozen" the check that I gave him for the car and so it hadn't cleared. They were angry and yelling that they were going to call the cops on us while my mother and I apologized for my father's stupidity. I was furious with my father because of this but it didn't stop me from looking for a car.

I finally found a blue 1987 Chrysler Fifth Ave for $800 in Rhode Island. My friend George agreed to drive me down there. I made sure that this time I paid in cash for it so it would be a final sale. I drove it home, and I was so proud. My father wasn't happy about it (surprise surprise), and again he kicked it and kicked me for buying it. I didn't care though; I knew that a car was my ticket to freedom in high school as it is for most teenagers. I remember it was a Friday when I drove it home, and the plates wouldn't be ready until Monday. But my friends and I wanted to drive it right away. So, Jose and I along with my brother-stole plates off another car that we noticed had never been driven and put them on my car. I remember that Friday night was my first night of freedom with my friends- Jose, Giuseppe, George and Spunge. We drove around to Walmart where we would steal shit. I stole disposable cameras and accessories for my car. We spent a lot of time at Old Country Buffet. Sometimes we snuck in when we didn't have money, and literally filled our pockets with hot fried chicken then walked out! Yes, those were some good times. All that was missing now was girls…

FOOTBALL CAMP and NHEC

In the summer of 2000 before I went into my junior year, my father signed me up for the National Hispanic Environmental Council's summer program for Hispanic teens. I don't want to talk too much about it, except let you know that I absolutely fell in love with the nature in Glorietta, New Mexico as well as Santa Fe —and the people that I will never forget. I found out from this trip that people loved my sense of humor—I was funny, and I loved being praised for it. We had hotel rooms that we shared so I met people from all over the country.

I must say that my favorite memory of it was when they gave us a private tour at night at Pueblo National Park. There was nothing but the sound of crickets, and a full starlit sky. We were all very quiet sitting outside in the field; then, all of a sudden, we heard the Anasazi Indians chanting, and you saw the Pueblos dancing with torches. I swear to you this was the most calming, Zen-like feeling that I had ever experienced. For some reason I teared up, thinking about my past, my dreams, and my future. I ended up with a love and appreciation for the Pueblo Indians and their ruins.

Another favorite night at the conference came when we were telling our story by the fire in the park at night. My friend Juan, who was from the streets of Los Angeles, told a story that made us all tear up. He talked about his best friend dying in his arms because after a drive-by. He and his friend were involved in with the Bloods and Crips gang wars in Los Angeles. As he spoke, tears rolled down his eyes, and he made me feel his pain, and cry with him. It was brutally honest but, as painful as Juan's story was, it was also beautiful at the same time.

FOOTBALL CAMP

In the last week of my summer going into junior year, we had football camp, where I played as a defensive tackle. I joined the junior varsity team. Anyway, my roommate was this overweight kid who eventually dropped out because of asthma. So I ended up with a single room.

I'm not gonna lie. Football camp for me was difficult again because of my high levels of anxiety. There were times when we were in a room before a game, and everyone was mingling while I just sat there not knowing who to talk to. Then one night, when everyone was out having fun and playing cards, I was depressed and in bed. As much as I wanted to be included with the football team, I was good at excluding myself. About halfway through the season, I was in the locker room at the high school and I'm about to open my locker to get my pads on right before practice starts. I discovered that someone had put a combination lock on my locker so that I couldn't access my pads and uniform. I was fucking angry and saddened that someone would do this to me. But I had a pretty good idea of who it was—probably one of the younger classmen who were in a grade below me. I never made a big stink about it, mainly because I was tired of fighting my way out of everything. I was just depressed, and I told Coach Lamb that I was quitting the team. I told him I needed time for my studies, and he was very understanding. That year, the Norwood Mustangs football team were the undefeated state champs, and everyone got rings, except me, because I had quit...

I remember a teammate calling me up and demanding that I give him the Nike Mustangs sweatpants and hoodies that had been given to each player. I was such a pussy that I agreed to, so he drove up to Windsor Gardens and took them from me, and drove off. That same kid was the one that was pushing me around on our graduation day—I believe he was drunk. I ran into him years later and found he had wound up becoming a State Trooper. Unbelievable. I did have some empathy for him; he had lost his brother in a car accident and I'm sure that had a big effect on him.

JUNIOR YEAR G/F

Junior year was probably one of my favorite years of high school. You never forget the music during the years where you begin getting "play" from girls and getting laid. I had a girlfriend, Megan and I was pretty happy. I had met her through George and his girlfriend, Becky. I went on a couple of double dates with them and then she would invite us back to her house in Norwood. Her parents were pretty liberal and kind, they knew when we came and they left to go to "sleep", not worrying about what kind of things we'd be doing. And we did some kinky shit. I remember when it was me, Megan, George, and Becky-we were all sitting down on her couch when Megan put a blanket over us, and both girls started giving their guy hand jobs. Becky was giving one to George, and Megan was giving me one. What would start out as going out on dates to movies and dinners at Friendly's and the 99 Restaurant would turn into making out and getting head in the back seat of my car "The Blue Goose," or even the movie theater! Things got even more hot when we went back to her home where we'd do everything apart from sex.

One cold winter night I came home around 11pm on a Saturday night from Megan's house and my father came out of the house in his underwear and his leather belt chasing angrily after me! The guy was legit insane. It was snowing for Christ sakes! He chased me down the stairs and whipped me with the belt as I fell down an icy, snowy hill. I spent that night at Jose's house. I remember I was so sick and tired of his shit. Why was he acting like this towards me? I remember I even asked him why he would hit me and treat this way, but he just told me to shut up and get out of his face. It didn't work trying to talk to him. One day I finally had enough of his ways. He kicked me out of our house and so I left and arrived at Jose's house with nothing but a toothbrush. Both of his parents were incredibly welcoming as they understood my situation, and the father told me that I was welcome to anything I want. He honestly made me a little emotional—I didn't receive this kind of love from home. I stayed at Jose's house for about a week; we would play on his PlayStation console and I met his younger brothers—they were all so humble and polite. It was great spending time with Jose and his family. I felt like I was on cloud nine, staying with my best friend but reality came crashing down after about a whole week of being there, when there was a knock on the door. It was my parents along with my brother. We kind of just stood there looking at each other, and my mother as always, looked worried. After about twenty seconds, my father grabbed me and started cursing at me in Spanish in front of Jose; then he kicked me and made me leave with. In the coming weeks I would spend nights at the homes of other friends, including Spunge. Spunge was very accommodating and gave me everything that I needed to make my stay comfortable.

    I can trace my drinking problem to about the age of 16, when I'd began to drink a lot. One day we were all at Megan's house, I was drunk and I made her cry. George (aka Pilgrim) told me that I was "an asshole in his book," for making Megan cry, and they tried taking my car keys away from me—but I had a spare underneath the car. I took it, without them knowing, and drove away before anyone could stop me. The truth is that, during that time, I was a different man-I was so full of anger and wanted to have a "player like" persona with the ladies. I had no idea how I had made her cry, but I apologize. I didn't treat women with the respect that they deserved back then, probably because I had grown up watching my father and the way he treated my mother.

JUNIOR YEAR

Junior year was also when we began partying a lot; one night Jose threw a party at his house for the six of us. We used to stand outside of liquor stores and wait for people to buy us liquor, or call up J'juan Cherry. But in this case since Mr. Cherry wasn't available, we bought a bunch of beer and Captain Morgan (the liter handle) from someone else. Jose's parents were out of town that night. I remember I always associated with the idea that the more a person could drink, the more of a man it made him. What a dumbass I was! Anyway, I remember drinking about half a liter of the Captain Morgan rum—I was absolutely fucking drunk out of my mind-to the point where I had to pray to God to not let me die that night. I threw up all over myself, so Jose took off my pants and I remember I was in my boxers having been put outside in case I threw up again. They also put shinpads on my legs so that I wouldn't get cut up on the concrete. I remember Ming coming, and taking pictures of me fucked up. He did it purely to make fun of me, though he claimed that he did it so I'd have the memory of it. Jose took the camera away from Ming as he thought it was wrong and so did I. Ming was cunning and manipulative, he was incredibly smart but I did have to call him out on all of his bullshit sometimes. I survived that experience, but I kept trying to tell them to call an ambulance because

I thought I needed to have my stomach pumped. They wouldn't though, because they were all afraid of getting arrested for underage drinking. Honestly, looking back it was extremely irresponsible of Jose not to call an ambulance, because I could have easily died that night...

During this year, Ming would pick us up in his little blue Dodge Neon and we would go riding. When we were bored we'd go egging or tee pee houses, all that stuff. We spent a lot of time at 1A Pizza and Sub Shop eating their delicious steak and cheese subs. We also spent a lot of time going to the Chinese buffet in Canton, which isn't there anymore. But when junior year started and Giuseppe got his license, we all loved to hang with him in his black Pontiac Grand Prix.

My relationship with Megan was going nowhere fast. I told her that I loved her—as if you know what love is at 16! But we were slowly sinking. I remember we all went to the mall once; there were seven of us in the Blue Goose and, as we were driving we were all thinking that we were cool, drinking cans of Bud Light, including me, the driver. When we got to the mall I was joking around and laughing with the guys, when Becky came up to me and said that Megan wanted to talk to me. When I went over to talk to her, she didn't wanna talk. I said, fine, and walked back to my group of guys that I was having fun with. My feeling was that I didn't need this shit, I was having fun with my friends.

A little later, I started getting paranoid that she was cheating on me with my friend Jeff. I spoke to both her and him about it and she said that she wasn't. But when I saw them talking together I got really jealous and paranoid. Anyway, the relationship ended when I was passed a note from Becky in science class from Megan, who said she wanted to break up. We had only been dating a few months, but I felt bittersweet about the whole experience. I was a bit hurt but at the same time I didn't really care about her as I had much bigger problems to worry about. We came from two different worlds.

ESCOBAR WANNABEES

Sometime during the summer before senior year toward the end of high school, I began heavily experimenting with marijuana and started dealing it with Pablo. What started off with buying ounces and just selling grams and eighths, but expanded soon to quarter pounders of marijuana. We kept our thousands of dollars of cash in a red toolbox that we kept in the closet, and we were selling big. At first it was exciting to have this kind of money and power—it felt good whenever someone called up my Nokia cell phone-I thought I was so cool because I supplied the product and had developed this tough guy persona. It gave me a rush of excitement but nothing good can last forever, as we later learned.

Our supply ran dry, and we had to reach out to these men who I suspected were trouble, Marquis and Tyrone. At first, they gave us some hydro weed that was absolutely incredible—it had to be laced with something. But then, when it came time to get more, I told my brother not to give them the $350 that they were charging -I had a very bad feeling about them and didn't trust them. However, my brother didn't listen to me and gave them the money. As it turned out, they were ducking our calls and avoiding us. They had robbed us of the money. I remember walking the train tracks with my brother and being so mad at him that I punched him in the face.

I went to where Marquis lived with his girlfriend Kim and banged on their door. Kim opened it and told me that Marquis wasn't home. I was so angry that I yelled at the top of my lungs, "You're lying... where is he?! Where is he?!" She began to cry that she didn't know. I left but I yelled at her so intensely that you could see that the woman was traumatized. I didn't care, I was angry. We never did business with Marquis and Tyrone again. One day however, Tyrone pulled out a gun on Pablo and robbed him of our money. My brother, robbed at gunpoint! From that point on, we didn't play around. Although we had no access to guns at the time, we armed ourselves with pepper spray and switchblade butterfly knives just in case we encountered any problems.

The drug game was stressing me out; it's not easy at all. There's a thin line between being loved and being feared and you need to learn to balance that in order to be a successful drug dealer. We were fucking amateurs; I was the angry one and Pablo was the more rational one when it came to dealing with our problems with the drug dealing.

We got robbed a second time by our trusted connect, Ivan and Oleg. They were brothers, from the Ukraine with whom we dealt with for at least a year; we had put a lot of trust in them. That's another lesson: Don't ever trust anyone in this business. Keep your eyes open and be alert to your surroundings. Anyway, as I was saying, I gave $300 to Ivan and Oleg, and they willingly took it and were supposed to get me an ounce ... only they never did. A few weeks passed and the same thing happened that had with Marquis and Tyrone—they were avoiding us and our phone calls. This time, I planned on getting revenge on Ivan.

We were out looking for them one Friday night; was my brother and I, and Aleksey, driving around Norwood in his black Mitsubishi

Eclipse. My brother called him and asked what he was doing that night, and we were able to figure out that he was in a car driving around town. When we finally saw the car, we cornered them and high beamed the car, forcing it to stop. Immediately I spotted Ivan in the backseat. I got out of my car and quickly moved toward their car, opened the back door and pulled out Ivan who was high (surprise surprise). My brother followed behind me. I pulled him out, threw him on the ground, and beat the fucking daylights out of him. I was punching with all I had, kicking and screaming at him. This was the first time I had ever beaten anyone up, and I wanted to make it count. I had so much anger held in from what my father was doing to me that I just exploded, and took it all out on him. I didn't even know what was happening; all I heard in the background was some girls screaming, and so was Ivan—the biggest girl of all. Then I heard Pablo yell, "Jan, we gotta go, the police are coming!" Another girl had called the police, and now they were looking for a black Mitsubishi eclipse. I did not want to get in trouble, and so I had to think fast. As we hopped back into the car I called Jose, and told him to pick us up so that my brother and I could change cars so the police wouldn't be able to find us. Jose picked us up somewhere near his house near Norwood Center, and we switched cars into a Chrysler minivan. We said goodbye to Aleksey as he drove away and hopped into the minivan. Jose came through for me. I was so happy that he picked up my brother too. The police were on the lookout but they wouldn't find us now because we were in a different car. We drove around town and saw multiple cop cars passing by with their sirens on. When Jose drove by my apartment complex later on that night, there were at least 20 of Ivan's friends waiting for me to get home so they could kick my ass. They were all in the front entrance, so my brother and I went in from the back, which they didn't have access to us. We were frightened and constantly looking out to window to see if the guys had left. Finally, they did, and my brother and I went to sleep in the small room that we shared on our twin size mattresses.

The next day, at school, people asked if I had been in a fight but I wouldn't answer. Finally, I saw my brother who told me that Ivan had bruises and marks all over his face. He looked black and blue. He had also told Pablo, "Your brother is dead." I was just happy that I had been able to stand up for myself. He deserved every punch that I threw. I was content with everything that had happened. I felt hat people would look at me and fear me; they would now respect me and not fuck with our business.

RELAY FOR LIFE

One very embarrassing moment for me in high school was the end of junior year, when we had our relay for life, an event to fundraise money for cancer. Anyway, about eight of us were all in a tent, and Ming was making fun of me saying that I was so excited about some girl that I began "shooting the roof." He was referring to a time where I prematurely ejaculated with Megan. Hey, it happens. Point is, I should have never shared with that information and I pretended to fall asleep instead of saying something back. Another friend, Becky, said in pity, "Jan stand up for yourself." I'll never forget that night, it made me feel so small. I remember Demetrius saying to me, "Your own friends don't even respect you." I'll never forget that night...

MEET THE DEVIL

One night I was at a neighbors small party when I encountered John Thomas; the memory of this man would become a nightmare that has haunted me to this day. John was an older man, about 50ish. He dressed in all black, listened to heavy metal and believed in the devil: weird shit like that. He lived in the same apartment complex as me. One night, sometime in the summer before my senior year, I was at his house and we were all smoking marijuana and drinking. Now, marijuana for someone who has mental illness is not a good idea, because it can make you more paranoid and more fucked up than everybody else at the party. I was out of control—I smoked way too much to the point where I had to leave. As I left the party, I picked up a bottle of Jack Daniel's Whiskey which I should never have touched. I was hammered and high, and I passed out in my home. My father wasn't home. My mother began showing me pictures of me when I was a child and crying. Not exactly sure how this would help the situation, but that's how my mother was. Anyway, the next day, I tried to call John to return the bottle, I even put it back on his front door and left a nice letter apologizing. He didn't care. He avoided me for about two months—I didn't see him at all. He just texted me threats that he'd kill me. This was a scary time for me. Ming gave me this Chinese knife—it was long and sharp and looked like a traditional samurai sword, sort of comical. At this point I was extremely fearful and carried it on me. It's important to understand that during this point I was extremely paranoid as well as depressed about life—I was suicidal even; I often had thoughts of killing myself. From what was going on at home to the drug dealing business, and now this, it was too stressful—too much pressure to take. I had no one to turn to and nowhere to run... I was stuck somewhere where I didn't want to belong. I was walking around depressed as well as paranoid and anxious, with Ming's samurai sword tucked in my pocket. I was so worried and distracted that one day the guidance counselor had to pull me out of class because I had left my car running—I had forgotten to shut it off!

One day, as I was waiting for the train at the Windsor Gardens platform, I was hanging out on the bridge when all out of nowhere, John showed up and pulled a big long sharp hunting knife to my left cheek. Who seriously carries around a hunting knife and why have there been so many incidents involving sharp knives in my life?! As he pushed in the knife he began swearing at me and saying "I should fucking kill you. I should fucking kill you, you piece of shit!" As he was saying this I went into shock—I don't know if you have ever been threatened with a knife before, but it's pretty scary. I completely froze and went into shock. He didn't end up killing me, obviously—but he pressed the knife right into my cheek and left me with a small cut from the knife. My neighbor was there with another guy, I remember the guy telling me to pick up that rock and smash his face in, but I couldn't do it. I was too scared of what might happen. So I did the only thing that a tough guy drug dealer would do—I ran home and called the police. They ended up stopping the train in Dedham but didn't find him because the description I had given them was wrong!

The worst part was what happened the next day at school. Apparently, the incident had made the front page of the Norwood Bulletin, which is bullshit because they're not supposed to release a minor's name, which I was as I was only 17 at the time. Anyway, I was in math class when the teacher Mr. Tomasso began questioning me about it. Mr. Tomasso was this old Italian guy who thought he was cool cause he wore a fucking leather vest every.. .single... day. He wanted to know what had happened, and when I didn't want to talk about it, he persisted and asked if it was drug-related. I was so pissed at him; he was a fuckin dickhead, he didn't have to get into my business like that—after all, I was already in distress from this, now the whole school knew. People were coming up to me saying, "Hey you made the front page of the paper this morning!" These were people that I didn't even know, but they knew me now.

SENIOR PARTY

Senior year came finally at Norwood High and my parents left for Poland to handle "important family matters" leaving my brother and I all alone for two months. This was one of the most difficult periods of my life, because they didn't leave us much money for food and I didn't even know how to do laundry! So one day, in class, we were talking about having a small get together on the Friday night, when all of a sudden, all of my classmates began talking about have a party at my house and coming over. So I replied, sure, why not, after all-my parents were away. Well, I was expecting around 10 people to show, but over 40 showed up! At first it was Megan and Becky, Erica and Erin and my crew George, Jose, Giuseppe, Ming and Spunge. Pablo (my brother) was there as well as his friends Sergei and Yuri. Later however, it was a madhouse in there! I went to smoke my hydro marijuana with a couple of people and couldn't stop coughing! Some people looked worried, while others just annoyed with all of my coughing. The marijuana made me extremely paranoid, and for some reason I started kicking people out. My brother was there and he was the only one that really looked out for me when no one else did. One kid, wouldn't leave and so I pushed him out the door and, when he tried to get back in, but I pushed hard and closed it and then locked it on him. He and

I were cool but we weren't close. Sometimes I'd give him rides home, though. He always seemed lost, with no direction to go in life. He was troubled just like I was. Many years later, I'd come to find out he'd been locked up for assault. He had randomly attacked some civilians in the Norwood Town center.

During the time my parents were gone, another thing that happened to my brother and I was that our house got robbed. I'll tell you how it happened. These guys named Darnell, Aiden and Craig came over the apartment supposedly to chill and hang out with my brother. I was going to 6 Flags amusement park with Aleksey when they came over. I said goodbye to everyone but I felt something wasn't right about that day. After about 10 minutes of driving I got a call from Pablo. He told me that Aiden and Craig had held him down while Darnell robbed our PlayStation, games, and my big book of CDs. This was serious, my parents were no involved and unfortunately so were the police.

Another time in senior year, my brother and I made a deal with a loser named Taylor . We went out and the plan was that we were going to meet him in the hills by the elementary school off 1A, but just as my brother and I had predicted, Taylor along with like 6 people ambushed us. They wanted to rob us and tried to jump us. This was the first time I saw my brother really kicking ass. He was a judo champion and knew how to take care of himself if things got rough. I saw him flipping guys this way and that way; he handled three people at a time! I didn't want anyone to get hurt, so when two guys came at me I wrestled them down to the ground. We were close to 1A and I wanted to attract as much attention to our fight as possible, so that someone could stop it or help us, so I threw my bike on 1A to stop traffic and continued with our fight. All of a sudden, my brother looked at me and said, "Jan, should I do it?" He was referring to the pepper spray that I had illegally gotten from some security guard. Desperate times call for desperate measures, and of course I told my brother to mace Taylor, so he did. After he was maced and crying, my brother Pablo and I ran all the way back to our house. I said goodbye to Pablo, and I went to work at the Dunkin Donuts in South Norwood. About an hour later, a detective came by to talk to me about the pepper spray incident,. I denied everything. I told him that I had been at work, so I had no knowledge of what happened.

He went to our apartment on Engamore Lane in Windsor Gardens later, while I was at work, to speak to my parents. He told them that he thought that Pablo and I were dealing drugs and that they were onto us. He knew about the robbery and he knew about the pepper spray incident. That shit wasn't our fault though—they tried to jump us, so if anything we were just protecting ourselves.

LOSING MY VIRGINITY

I had been working a lot and saving up money at the Dunkin Donuts at the Shell Gas Station on Route 1A. I would always hook up all my friends who came in. Mainly a dozen donuts and coffee. I'd also steal these coupon books that my boss had in the desk where he thought they were safe. It was Dunkin Cash, and each coupon was a dollar. I had about $500 worth of these, and kept them stashed in my red toolbox in my closet in my brother and I's room.

I remember one day I was really sleepy so my manager sent me home. I thought I was alone and I fell asleep on my mattress in my room. Next thing I knew, I heard the front door unlock and there was my father, he started yelling at me wondering why I was home and not at work. He immediately kicked me out and yelled at me to go back to work! I didn't go back to work; I couldn't go in the state that I was in. I felt so abandoned, like no one loved me nor cared about what I was going through at home. So I went to our apartment complex's community fitness center, and did what any normal person would do—I fell asleep on the floor by the weight bench. Some Indian guy walked in and was shocked to discover me as I lay sleeping on the carpeted floor. I knew that something was off for me to be sleeping on a cold carpet in our apartment complex's fitness center. I didn't feel safe and I didn't feel comfortable. The Indian man was the one that woke me up; I was a bit embarrassed, and I left immediately.

Although my ex-girlfriend was the only person that I was experimenting with sexually but never went all the way- I could've had sex with her one time when she came over to my house but it never happened. I have no clue why I didn't do it. But, I did lose my virginity at 17 after a girl named Tarea, came into Dunkin Donuts, and we began flirting. This girl was beautiful! She had a nice shaped body and a cute face. I wanted her bad. What started as innocent flirtation led to her coming by the shop every day just to see me... and get her coffee. Soon I invited her out in the back and we would be making out among other things behind closed doors. Eventually I invited her over to my house when my parents weren't home and that was my first time. I'll never forget it. We started out kissing then we both got naked and she told me to put on a condom—I did. Then she asked if I wanted to do it doggystyle. I did. I entered her from the back and began to fuck her hard. She was incredibly wet and tight, and I enjoyed it. She wanted to be my girlfriend, but I didn't want to be tied down, especially since I was going to Bridgewater State in the fall. So I eventually said let's just be friends.

SENIOR CLASS TRIP: MONTREAL

For our senior class trip sometime in March of 2002, only two months away from graduation, me, Giuseppe, Ming, and George decided to room together. We boarded a bus from the Walpole Mall, and everyone was hammered on that bus. It's funny, when you see your classmates drunk it's completely different to the way they behave than when you see them in class! The guys were much more emotional, some were angry, some were even crying, but one thing was for sure, it was an interesting bus ride!

Anyway, graduation was approaching and I didn't give a fuck—I was known as trouble, since everyone seemed to know about my "business," and we were gonna go all out on this trip to Montreal. Once we got to the hotel, the first thing we did was go to a strip club. We also really enjoyed buying LeBeau Beer from the shops in the city and drinking in public on the streets at age 17. It was all legal in Montreal! When we went to the strip clubs, in order to be seated you had to tip the bouncer or he'd literally put his hands on you and kick you out. They took advantage of us real good; they thought we were just kids and could be pushed around. I remember kissing strippers while we got private lap dances, and at night we would go to Mansion, Montreal's hottest nightclub where I hooked up with a girl and spent the night making out on the dance floor. She was already hammered, and I could've taken her home, but instead what did I do—buy her more beer. I didn't know any better, and so we continued doing our thing on the dance floor. The whole trip was a giant shit show—we were all so fucking hammered during the three day trip, mostly going from strip club to strip club...and the strippers were rude at one club-they wanted us to leave because we weren't throwing them money on stage! But at night after the trips to the clubs it was terribly cold, and often I wasn't wearing a jacket. I saw another drunk teen get beat up and I noticed he was bleeding from his nose and so I assisted him and asked him if he was okay. Another time, something in the food that I ate made me sick and I remember throwing up all over the street! After one club, I checked in my jacket and they wouldn't give it back because I had lost the ticket. Ming actually helped me with that when they asked what I had in the jacket pocket. I couldn't figure it out I was so drunk, until Ming told me it was my hat! So I thanked him and finally got my jacket back.

I was a smart ass who refused to listen to anybody but myself. I was extremely stubborn, wanting to do everything my way. Going back as we boarded the bus, I hid a 1 liter bottle of vodka in my bag. When we got to the Canadian border, they did a thorough check and brought out German Shepherds and all kinds of cool shit. Turns out that they found my bottle of vodka. I had to tell them it was mine. I really didn't know what kind of trouble I was getting myself into. The facts were: I was a minor as they found out when they checked my ID. I had no clue what was going to happen. They took me to a room and they told me to dump out the liquor, and I did. Everyone on the bus was shocked to see me taken away by border patrol and his sniffing K9. I sat in the office for about half an hour and they asked me if I had anything else that they should know about and if I knew the severity of the punishment for what I had just done. I spent about 30 minutes in that room but thank God nothing bad happened and they allowed me to go back on the bus and home back to Massachusetts.

RACIST MATH TEACHER

Back at home in Norwood, everyone was excited that school was almost over and in an upbeat mood. But I had people that didn't want me to graduate, like the dickhead math/computer teacher Mr. Amati, who wanted to fail me and prevent me from graduating with the rest of the class. I also took a computer course as an elective with him, during senior year. He had sat me down one day after class, looked me in my eye and asked me, "Jan, are you a criminal? Do you do criminal activity?" I was shocked but I knew that he had all the power in his hands to deny me my high school diploma, and so I said innocently, "No, I'm not; I'm a good guy that just wants to graduate!" I'm not sure if he believed me, but I do know that he had no right to ask me that, the racist fuck. I hated him, I hated everything about Norwood High, which was full of racist kids and teachers. The majority of the student population was white, mainly Irish and Italian kids. From Mr. Tomassi wanting me to publicly discuss the incident earlier that year with the knife to Mr. Amati grilling me about me being a criminal, I had had enough of this shit. I told him what he wanted to hear, but I wasn't happy, and I would never forget this.

One day, I believe it was the last week in Mr. Lyons English class, while we were walking to class, a bully that had been teasing me all year had something smart to say—I was tired of all the bullshit and so I punched him in the face, and his reaction? He began tearing up as he said to me, "Why'd you do that?" Like he didn't fucking know? Again, this goes out to all the kids that get bullied—all I had to do was stand up for myself, it took one punch, and the kid began tearing up like a little bitch. I was thinking to myself, had I known that earlier it could've saved me a lot of grief and embarrassment. Fuck everybody that was against me, I was graduating and I was very proud of it!

When they called my name at graduation I heard all my classmates shout out and cheer "Pufffff!" I was proud-I survived those four years of hell—I bet many wouldn't be able to, but I did because, well… I've endured much worse pain in my life than four years of high school. I graduated Norwood High School Class of 2002.

PROM 2002

Prom was nearing and the girl that I originally asked was already going with someone. My ex told me that she'd go with me to prom but I had no desire to go with her. I had no date until the last minute, when Jose suggested that I should ask out this girl Shannon Fitzgerald, who was two years younger than me. I had met Shannon when she hung out in Windsor Gardens, and I wanted to go with a stunningly beautiful girl-and so I picked her. Shannon had blonde hair and beautiful blue eyes, and looked amazing in her pink dress. It was prom day, and I picked out my tuxedo with a silver vest. We all met up at Giusseppe's house. Then we picked up our dates and drove in our rented limousine to the Copley Plaza Hotel in Boston. Spunge tried to sneak a 30-pack of Budweiser into the limo and when the limo driver looked at him and Spunge was like "hey! You don't mind do you?" The guy was serious about his job and told us that since we were underage we couldn't bring in the booze. It wasn't the greatest start.

When we got to the Copley Plaza Hotel we took pictures of the guys and then just us individually with our prom dates. I still have my picture; I don't even know what kind of pose I was doing to be honest. It looks like I'm trying to show off and be arrogant, but I just came out looking stupid with my fish lips. The prom was overwhelming. Everyone was just in a giant circle and socializing—I didn't like that one bit, and so I stuck by my friends, or at least I tried to. I didn't really like my date; I had only picked her because she looked good, but she was being incredibly stuck up and not dancing with me but mingling with her friends instead. I was angry, and on my pictures you can see that I had a rather angry and upset face. I didn't appreciate her acting like this as I had to pay for all her shit . But I did have fun and dance with Spunge and Jose and my friends.

At the end our night me, Jose and Spunge all went to Jose's house, where we went over to a field of satellites in the middle of the night and got high, talking about the last night together of our high school days, and reminiscing. It was really a beautiful thing. It was the last time that we'd see each other for a while. I felt bittersweet about Norwood High, but like Charles Dickens said, "It was the best of times and the worst of times." I had terrible times in high school but also some of the best times of my life. In the fall I'd be starting at Bridgewater State College and Spunge would be going to Wentworth, while Jose would be working.

In August, just before starting my first year of college at BSC, my family went to stay at a motel somewhere in Maine. Things were extremely tense with my father, and because I got the towels wet he began arguing with me and spit in my face. He went overboard and it set me off. I began shouting about how much I hated him and how happy I was to be going to BSC so that I would never have to see him again. I told him that I only wanted to see mom and my baby bro Pablo, but that he could go fuck himself for all I cared. The last four years of high school had been hell for me, and instead of helping me he had just made everything worse with all the abuse and the militaristic style of parenting that he had.

FRESHMAN YEAR @ BSC SEPTEMBER 2002

It was September 2002, and I was finally going to BSC. On the first day, people were moving computers and laptops and all kinds of furniture and snacks, and I honestly didn't have much. I had spent all summer saving for an awesome HP Laptop, which was my prized possession. In fact, it was my only possession, along with one of those eggshell things you put under your mattress. As we walked through the halls of Shea Hall on "The Hill," my father was looking around at all the college freshmen, especially the ladies and being embarrassing while my mother egged him on. Of course I was uncomfortable and wanted them to leave immediately.

I'm not sure why I agreed to this, but I was in a triple dorm, meaning I'd share a room with two other guys. When we arrived on the 4th floor of Shea Hall, I met my first roommate, Chris, who was openly gay. He seemed pleasant, but I will be first to admit I was a little bit homophobic at times because of the close quarters. My other roommate, Dan, was a good Portuguese kid, from New Bedford I believe. They both seemed cool, although I immediately fit in more with Dan than the other roommate.

On our first night at BSC, we went to the cafeteria together and Becky from my high school linked up with us. I didn't have anything against her, but at the same time I had come to Bridgewater State for a new life-to meet and make new friends and she followed us around like a puppy everywhere we went. So I decided to break away from them. I knew that if I spent all my time with them I'd never meet other people. I was timid, and shy especially of girls. My roommate Chris had beautiful girls in our dorm all the time, and they liked me. I realized that if I didn't break out of my shell and learn to talk to girls I'd be spending the next four years having no wild sex while playing Warcraft or board games on weekends instead of going out and meeting new people. Things would have to change. I, along with my roommate Dan, organized the Shea Hall flag football league. I remember we printed ads with the information it would be every Monday and Wednesday from 6-8pm on the lawn in front of our dorms. This ended up turning out extremely successful as most of the students who joined our league were hot girls from our dorms, so I met some gorgeous girls.

I played quarterback and I loved it. Football was where I met my new best friend Danny. Danny was a skinny and reserved Haitian guy, who I began to hang out with. Immediately I learned that he was extremely loyal, and a good guy. There was something very different about Danny. He came from a broken home just like I did. He lived on campus like me, but he lived in Boston and he'd take the commuter rail to and from the school from Boston carrying his clothes in a large black trash bag. He lived with his schizophrenic mother. This is exactly why Danny would end up becoming my best friend through the next couple of years-because he was fucking real, at a time when not many people were. Danny understood that we were best friends and would do anything for me as I would for him.

Like me, he was broken, had came from poverty, and loved hip hop and Chinese food so we clicked instantly.

Next, I met Danny's roommate Alan, in their dorm room across campus in Scott Hall. Alan was a big white guy from Attleboro who tried way too hard to fit in. He was a bass player who thought he was cool because he was in a band. We called in him Baloo, as in the bear from Disney's the Jungle Book because, well, he was shaped like a big bear. Anyway, we all became friends. I would push the envelope and force myself to talk to girls, no matter how uncomfortable I got I had to learn to push through the anxiety. So I started to go to other girls dorms that I had met from our football league. I tried to get Alan to drive us to Providence and Boston to nightclubs, and parties. One of the best perks of being friends with Alan was that he had a car, and we could go anywhere, not just stay on campus. I remember one night we were in Providence, and I started talking to these girls who were smoking in their car, and I just hopped in and partied with them. I know, I couldn't believe how smooth I was when I was manic either! In my teens and in my 20's I LOVED going clubbing. I loved the music the drinks and the women. We would frequent nightclubs often. Alan had something that I wanted—these computer speakers that I could easily hook up to my HP laptop and play my hip hop loud. The thing about me is, I loved being the DJ. I knew more about hip hop than anyone and that's how I connected with people from my dorm. They'd like a song and walk into my dorm room and ask, "Hey I love that song, who is it by?" I had a friend named C-Los. He was a cool quiet Puerto Rican guy in my dorm that would get me new hip hop music before it even came out! I just loved college!

So I met a few cute girls from our football league, Emily, Liz, Jenna, Megan, Danielle, Alanna, Annette, Amara to name a few.

I also met some good friends like my Antonio, Bob, Darnell, Butz, Dan Dicenso (who would later be my best man), as well as Derron, who lived in the senior apartments.

I would later hang out with Megan and her roommates Amara and Annette, we all became close friends, but I developed the biggest crush on Megan. I became infatuated with her, she was short, and thick in all the right places, and had a great body. But what I loved most about Liz, was her smile. I tried to get with her many times and just kept getting rejected. She was giving me mixed signals, first that she was into me, and then that she wasn't into me. I learned from the "players" of BSC, that I needed to play hard to get to get her. "You see, the best way I can explain it is, women want what they can't have," my friends Derek and Edison, who were in the Sigma Chi fraternity would tell me. I met Edison through the Latino club at school and met Derek through Edison. Edison was a caramel-complexioned brother. He was Dominican, and spoke slowly in a low tone. Women found him mysterious, because of the way he carried himself. Derek was a Portuguese self-proclaimed "playboy" who loved the ladies and spent a lot of time bragging and telling us what he thought women wanted. Both of them were suave with the ladies, dressed well, and wanted me to pledge with them to the Sigmi Chi fraternity. Then there was my other good friend Charles, who was from Nigeria and loved Michael Jackson, just like I did. Charles was a cool guy; he was goofy but suave, and loved to dance like MJ. We instantly became friends. A lot of these people I met when I decided to join a college club called the Men Integrated in Brotherhood. I also met Stan in this group. Stan was the most chill, calm and happy person I've ever met. He was always fucking happy! I always asked him what he took to made him so chill cause I wanted it. I also met people through other clubs when

I joined the Latino club, the Cape Verdean Association. The thing is, these people, all had one goal, which was to bag women like groceries, and I wanted the same thing. So we all hung out together, shopped at similar places like Express for Men and the Gap. I started taking pride in the way that I looked like I never had in my life. I began running to relieve stress and maintain a good physique. I wanted to be cool, just like they were, and known for getting girls, being good with the ladies, and being a player. And so I embodied this style wherever I went. Freshman year of college was where I evolved from being the shy ugly duckling into the handsome fucking swan! I was proud of who I was and I hit on girls every chance I got. We all communicated on AOL Instant messenger and I loved chatting with everyone because I could post away messages and express to people how I was feeling at the time. It was also great for booty calls. If you were lonely one weekend and a girl friend was staying at the school you could message her to come watch a movie with you and in the middle of the night she would come over to your dorm or you'd go over to hers.

My father had taken me to the IT Help Desk at the Moakley Center at BSC and told the people there that I was new on campus and needed a job. Right away, they hired me on the spot as a IT Help Desk guy in the main computer lab. Now the funny thing is, I didn't know shit about fixing computers or hard drives, but you learned quickly. I liked the job but missed my friends. Megan and Amara and the gang would come visit me and a lot of the times I'd leave my shift early, without telling anyone I was going. I'd eventually get fired for this. But, on the plus side, I met this one girl Susana, who was thrilled to speak to me every chance she could. We became friends, and I found out one day from her that she needed to get laid. Susana looked like an enthusiastic, horny girl who would talk to me a lot in the computer lab as she worked in a different department in the Moakley Center. I knew that she was into me and somehow we ended up in a car I was driving that was borrowed at the time. We were in the parking lot of my dorm when all of a sudden, I leaned into her and we started making out. Then, I unzipped my jeans and I took out my cock and pulled her head towards it. She began to go down on me, in the parking lot of Shea/Durgin Hall on the Hill. It felt so good. Seeing her wild face going down on me got me extra horny. My only regret was that when we were all done I didn't invite her up for some late night sex and I'm not sure why I didn't. She was beautiful, and she was into me and I didn't fuck her. To this day I regret not taking her back up to my room.

Another good friend of mine was a Cape Verdean guy named Manny Centeio who was from Boston, and very business minded so we instantly became friends. Once a week, I would visit a psychologist down on Temple St in downtown crossing and we would talk about my anxiety and depression. This was actually the first time that I began to receive psychotherapy for my mental health issues. I was 18 years old. I would normally take the train from Bridgewater to South Station, and then the red line one stop to downtown crossing, where I'd get off and walk the rest of the way to my appt. The good thing with having Manny around was that he was a commuter, so after classes he'd drive me to Boston and drop me off at the LAZ parking garage where he worked as a supervisor. It was on State St, and from there I would walk the rest of the way. I'd take the train back from South Station back to Bridgewater; it was a time where I could be alone with my thoughts and just reflect on everything. I loved those train rides back to school. I didn't find my first therapist that good. I would sit there talking about how I was and the problems and stresses that I was going through and then ask him what he thought that I had (he mainly just stared at me as I spoke, observing me, and then told me that I had a "little anxiety and a little depression." Now, I have to tell you, that since I was an adolescent I absolutely loved psychology, and so the answer that that psychologist gave me told me that he really didn't have a deep enough understanding about what was going on with me. I KNEW that I had social anxiety disorder and I had a feeling that I had bipolar, because of my unstable moods and outbursts, and the mania, but at the time I wasn't really worrying about the bipolar as much as I worried about the social anxiety.

One of the things I thoroughly enjoyed about being in college is the freedom of it, and the fact that you had to be responsible for your own self and manage your time efficiently. You had to make sure you set the alarm for 7am in order to make it to classes and if you failed to do this, you wouldn't pass This all required discipline and, overall, the fact that I had to care for myself in school and look after myself made me much more responsible and confident in myself. I really loved meeting up with all my friends and going to the dining room for lunch and dinner, it was a lot of fun when everyone was friendly and in good spirits. It seemed like everywhere I had turned I had friends, and there was hardly ever a time where I had to sit alone. I know that's one of many young people's fears when they enter college: who they will sit with. They don't want to sit alone because they think they'll be perceived as a loser. It's good to step back from the crowd and find yourself during these years. Don't be afraid to venture off alone onto a different path from the rest of your peers. That's the best advice I could give to the young people out there reading my memoir. It's okay to be afraid; just use that fear to push yourself through whatever is causing you to feel afraid. It's also okay to be different. It's what makes us unique.

I joined group therapy for those with social anxiety at the school's counseling center, and also got regular therapy from a tiny, soft-spoken Asian man named Wayne who really helped me a lot. These therapy sessions were great because I met other guys in the same boat as me with the social anxiety, many of whom became friends. They were very supportive of me; when I spoke they listened and offered suggestions and when they spoke I did the same. A lot of them told me that they found it hard to believe that I had social anxiety, because I seemed like a fun outgoing guy and they didn't see that side of me. They thought of me as extremely outgoing and having many friends, But I did have extreme anxiety. The groups helped; it turned out that we had many similar fears and anxieties and we worked out our fears in therapy. I became close to a few of the people there, especially this guy James, who ended up going out with Susana.

That first semester as a freshman at Bridgewater State College was the best time of my fucking life! I fucked girls and partied a lot. I had a lot of friends, and would meet people through them. I dated girls from Wellesley College, and got invited to the Latina club dance parties in MIT and Wellesley and a couple of universities and colleges in Boston. I also partied with my best friend Spunge from high school. He was now at Wentworth Institute of Technology in the heart of downtown Boston, and we would go to parties all the time- in apartments, at different frat houses of MIT and Northeastern. Jose came along for the ride as well, and sometimes so did our friend George. I'd be drunk every weekend and was living the life! Girls, jello shots, and Beirut! Spunge was a true friend. Often he'd help my drunk ass get back into the Wentworth dorms and steal his roommate's Chinese food or whatever else was in their fridge just so I could eat. However, I'm not sure why, but I began being abusive to

Spunge. When I was drunk one time I remember playfully punching him and pushing his head in a snow bank. Jose would tell me that Spunge was fragile and I could really hurt him, and I didn't think that he was serious back then. But now I realize that I probably scared him.

Then there were the parties at Jose's house. There were girls there I would hook up with. One of them was a cute Irish girl named Colleen, who would later pass away-Rest In Peace. I had a lot of fun partying because I had a different swag about myself and the way I carried myself was different to how it had been in Norwood High School. I was the man and felt that I could get with any girl I chose. These girls saw that, and were eager to hook up. We'd sometimes see our old friends Giusseppe and Ming too, but they were less frequently in our lives now.

My other best friend, Aleksey also threw parties at his dorm. We would also go to other Russian house parties, where I would introduce myself as a charming and confident, slick young man. I had a dark side that could emerge when I drank though, and in this chapter in my life I still had a heart filled with hatred. I remember once I was drunk and hustled another guy who had thrown a party. The party was in Brighton or Chestnut Hill or somewhere and this Russian guy came from wealth. He showed off. So... I gave him daps and shook his hand as I slowly pulled of his class ring from high school off his finger. I then proceeded to go into his mother's bedroom and stole jewelry —a necklace and a watch. I was troubled and I needed help. I felt ashamed and was hiding my true self from others. I remember another time we were at some Northeastern house party in Mission Hill, a section of Roxbury off Huntington Ave so of course, I was drunk and we went into the bedroom with the party-goers coats on the bed. I told Danny to steal whatever he could find in those jackets—wallets, cellphones, condoms—whatever would be of value. I was supposed to be on the lookout for people passing by as Danny had his hands in coat pockets and purses. At first it was going well, but I kept drinking and wasn't paying attention, and the host of the party saw us trying to steal and he said we had to leave. I got into an argument with him, wanting to know why we were being kicked out, and he said, "you guys were stealing!" I played the race card and yelled that he was racist and was only kicking us out because my friend was black...It didn't work, of course.

My other friend Antonio introduced me to his roommate Bob, who was a big dork but a nice guy. I ended up going to a football game at Randolph High School where I met his beautiful sister, Joanna, who was a senior cheerleader at the time and had taken a liking to me. Joanna and I began to hook up and dated a few times. She would sneak down to visit me whenever she visited her brother Bob at the dorms, and we'd innocently make out. We were both 18 and I was having the time of my life, bro! She invited me to my first Spooky World experience, during Halloween season 2002. She found out that I was terrified of the clown house, and we held each other and kissed whenever her brother wasn't around her. We sat out on the hay; it was my first time seeing Billy Pickett sing "The Monster Mash". I loved that song; he was a legend, but I noticed that he didn't seem to be particularly happy performing. His energy was gone, and it wasn't fun watching him sing the song. He was in his 70's and I shook his hand after his performance. Billy Pickett ended up dying a few years later, but he made history with "The Monster Mash", and I'll never forget seeing him perform live. We ate candied apples and funnel cakes, and excitedly walked around Spooky World in our GAP hoodies on a chilly, fall evening. I loved it. It just felt so good, so surreal. I really enjoyed hanging with Joanna, but when her brother Bob found out that we were hooking up our friendship was compromised. He wanted nothing to do with me anymore and demanded that I stop dating his sister. I had no intention of stopping, I enjoyed spending time with her, but she respected her brother's wishes and stopped dating me. I had become friends with many women for the first time, and the more I believed that I was a ladies' man, the more I became one. The power of positive thinking baby! I also partied with Jenna and Robyn, who were both roommates. I idolized Jenna—she was everything that I wanted in a woman, absolutely stunning, pretty, short, and curvy in all the right places! Best of all though was that she liked to party. We would drink Bacardi 151 and run around the tennis courts drunk and shit. I wanted her so bad—I had to have her, even if she was sleeping around a lot on campus. Eventually I did hook up with her and we grew closer. More on that later.

Through those girls I also met Steve, who was this white kid from the burbs with whom I began buying Poland Spring water bottles filled with vodka. Although these were the best times of my life, I still felt alone-I had demons in me and I used alcohol as a way of "numbing the pain." I knew I had a problem. I loved to drink. Hell, I drank straight vodka out of that water bottle and began walking around the dormitory halls stumbling down the stairs, People didn't understand who I was, my struggle or where I came from—I couldn't relate to all the white suburban kids who had led happy lives. I wasn't happy with myself, especially all the trauma I had endured with my abusive father in my past. I believed that I was "broken" and couldn't relate to almost anyone with the exception of minorities. You see, minorities who looked like me came from similar backgrounds as me, therefore they could relate to the struggles that

I faced. That's he reason why I picked a state school, because there was a large minority population which meant I would feel more comfortable. For as long as I could remember I partied hard and was out of control with the alcohol. I felt alone out there on my own, and different than everybody else. I came from a different breed, and as much as there were friends who attempted to understand me, they couldn't help me.

I had taken all of my midterms and final exams, and before you knew it, the first semester of college was over, and I was going back home for winter break. I was happy to go home to see all my friends in Norwood and spend the holidays with them. Spunge got me a job at Ocean State Job Lot, where he and Jose worked. I believe during this time my mania was extremely high. I valued myself more and I demanded that my so-called high school friends respect me. If they didn't, I would not be afraid to leave them because I began to see that I could make friends easily and that they could be easily replaced. I told them that flat out. I needed them to respect me because, if they didn't, I'd stop hanging out with them.

During our one month winter break from school, I worked at Ocean State Job Lot. I'd wake up at 4:30, roll out of bed, hop on my bike and ride through South Norwood and through Dean St to get to work at 5 am then work until 1 pm. I also still kept in touch with the general manager at Dunkin Donuts, who gave me hours at a store near Ocean State, on Rt1, near where Honey Baked Ham was. The manager at Ocean State, Rich Haskell, motivated and inspired me to work with a strong work ethic. I took pride in beginning the hard work at 5 in the morning, and I loved the sense of community there. I began to realize that school was a waste of time, and that I was lost about the direction that I wanted my life to go. I was a Management Science major, but only because I put on this façade like I was a businessman, an entrepreneur who dreamed of owning Shell Gas stations and Subway franchises. I worked a lot, I saved up money for school and things that I would need because I had to pay for school on my own. I wasn't a privileged white kid whose parents footed their kids' tuition and other expenses.

During this time my brother was still selling weed and entangled in all that bullshit. I tried to steer clear of all that, but he was in it fully. He was known as a troublemaker in the Norwood community and had two criminal court cases pending. One night, he got into a physical fight with Charles, a guy from Africa who attacked my brother with a hammer and hit him in the head. My brother fought him, and they rolled down a big hill fighting. My brother came home and told us that he had just been hit in the head with a hammer. You could see a big bump on his forehead. I immediately grabbed a baseball bat and ran up with my brother's best friend Sergei, to Charles' house to beat the living shit out of him. The only thing is, he wouldn't open the door. Charles was a punk, we hated him. Years later we'd find out through mutual friends that he had been murdered in Boston. What goes around comes around.

My father did one very good thing for my brother to help save him from going to jail or, even worse, getting killed. He sent my brother to live on a farm in Ecuador with his family. My brother spent three months in Ecuador learning a little of the language, making fresh scrambled eggs with the eggs laid every morning from hens on the farm, and attending school there. All I have to say is, that when my brother Pablo came back from Ecuador, he was a changed person, and he had his head on his shoulders. Next, my father enrolled him in military school to get my brother some discipline. So in 2004, when my brother graduated Norwood High School, he would be going to Massachusetts Maritime Academy in

Buzzards Bay, Cape Cod. This school also transformed my brother into a leader.

In January of 2003 I returned to Bridgewater for spring semester of my freshman year. I was so happy to be back somewhere I felt like I was home now. It felt good to be around so many friends. This semester, I had accepted that Megan did not want me in a romantic way, so I became okay with just being her friend. We became very close; I was my natural goofy and dorky self around her and we spent a lot of time together. I stopped trying to romance her or any other of that bullshit, I stopped trying period. We were just friends. The thing I remember most is that I could make her laugh, just by being myself. We clicked so well together. We flirted so much it was almost impossible to believe that she didn't want me. We spent an awful lot of time together, and one Friday night in February of 2003, she invited me to drink with her. She supplied the alcohol and we began drinking in her dorm room. We were flirting and laughing and drinking and were being very touchy feely with each other, when soon enough I reached in and kissed her. She kissed back, and we started passionately kissing each other. We started hooking up and tearing off each others clothes. Finally we were both naked and in her bed. I sucked on her beautiful big soft tits with those tiny Braille pink nipples and got her off. I began to eat her out with my self proclaimed "hurricane tongue." Damn I was full of myself back then. She tasted so good, like some exotic sweet melon. All fucking year I had been trying to get with Megan, and now it was like the stars and the moon were aligned and shit and everything was going my way, everything was perfect. The thing is, I knew that she was a virgin so I did not have sex with her that night. The next morning my friend Edison came into her room and announced, "So, this is the new couple," with a smirk on his face. I felt like the man, and gave him a confident grin and replied, "why yes, yes we are." Megan didn't say anything. The next day, I was very affectionate with her—I was kissing her goodbye, walking her to class holding hands... it doesn't take an Einstein to see that this was a big mistake. As much as I was now on cloud nine and infatuated with Megan, the reality of the situation was that Megan didn't feel the same way. She wanted what had happened to be just a one-night stand, and nothing more. So, she began distancing herself from me.

I was incredibly hurt and angry. I couldn't understand why she would all of a sudden cut off all communication with me. We had been good friends and now she was pulling this on me? She began avoiding me at all costs and I didn't like it. Derek and Eddy told me to stay cool, and I tried for a while, but after a few weeks, I got drunk (surprise), went to her room and knocked on her door loudly, demanding that she open the door. I was absolutely obliterated as my friend Edison would say, and I began shouting at her late in the twilight hours of the night pouring my heart and soul out. What was I shouting? Let's just say I was unleashing all the anger that I had kept inside. I wanted her to feel the pain that I was feeling because of her actions. I called her a slut and told her that she was fake. I was using all sorts of profanities and I wasn't thinking about how I might hurt Megan. But my view is that you shouldn't lead a man on like that and have him fall for you and then the next minute ghost him like that. That's not right. I'm a moral person and to me, she just took advantage of my heart and crushed it. I don't mean to sound like a little bitch, but I'm a real type of dude and you don't mess with somebody's feelings like that. I had been yelling in a drunken rage, for about 20 minutes just hitting on the door and yelling, when her roommate Amara came out, and explained to me that this wasn't the right way to tell her how I felt. So eventually

I left. But I easily could have been arrested that night. It was the wrong way to behave and looking back it was really immature of me and I was acting like a total asshole.

A few days later she wrote me a letter apologizing for what she had done. She said that she had issues and because of her childhood she was afraid of being vulnerable and was extremely guarded. We ended up meeting in one of the common areas of the dorm and hashed it out. It was hard to get her to open up at first, but she got very emotional when she started talking about her father who had been absent most of her life, and how she had had to take care of her mother and little sister for a long time. She began crying, and I saw how broken Megan really was. She hid her pain well behind that beautiful smile. But I was able to crack her open, and finally see her truth at face value. We hugged it out and I felt more accepting of her apology knowing more about her story. I felt bad for her. Things were never the same between us, even though we agreed to remain friends. When me and Danny visited them to hang out, the atmosphere wasn't the same anymore.

Not gonna lie, I still wanted Megan to be mine, and I was heartbroken. I had become obsessed and infatuated with her. It got to the point where I got really crazy and needed another outlet to keep my mind busy. Derek told me that the best way to get over a girl is to keep busy, get a job. And so I did. I worked for a few months at the Dunkin Donuts at Bridgewater, sometimes as much as 30 hours a week, so that I could keep busy and not think about her. But it wasn't the end solution. I began to realize that I'm too much of a Captain Saver with women, that I get too many feelings and emotions involved, and that that just leads to me getting hurt by them. From now on I was going to protect my heart at all costs. So I became much colder with women. From then on, I wasn't going to be miserable. To me, women were evil creatures and, if they sensed that you were too nice or falling for them, they'd rip your heart out and serve it to you on a silver platter. I started sleeping with more women on campus and stopped sharing so much emotion about how I felt about a girl. If I liked someone, I teased them and was a bit of an asshole. You may think this is bullshit but let me tell you it works. I wanted to get Megan back, and I worked hard to win her back. I decided to do what any stand up guy would do and invite Jenna, one of my booty calls (as I'll explain below) to my room and invite Megan over at the same time so that they would meet each other. I was hoping to make Megan jealous by doing this, but she if she was she hid it well. Anyway, I never ended up getting Megan back, and our friendship never was the same again. You live and you learn, and what doesn't kill you makes you stronger.

As I said, I called Jenna, the girl that I had met in the first semester and partied with her and her roommate Robyn. Anyway, we were talking more and more on AIM and getting lunch together at the cafeteria. So one night, she messaged me, that she wanted to come down. By this point, I left my roommates we all decided it'd be best if I had a single room and I wanted it this way. I enjoyed having my own space and privacy, and it would be great to just be able to invite girls over to have sex with. One night Jenna came over well after midnight. She showed up at my door in her pajamas and told me that Robyn hadn't wanted her to come over. I didn't understand why at first, but just figured that Robyn wanted me for herself. Anyway, we proceeded to hooking up. She wanted me to fuck her raw. I was all for it because this girl was gorgeous, and I needed to mount her. So I did. Later on, I found out from another friend that he had fucked her right before I did! I was shocked and panicked at the same time. He asked me if I wore protection, and

I replied no. I fucked her raw. He told me that she gets around and that I should probably get tested. I was nervous as hell, I thought that I had caught something. I went to the doctor and I got tested; I don't ever want to go through that again. I'm not sure if you know how they test men for STD's, but they take a cotton swab and stick it into your penis. It really hurts and that's one memory I never want to relive again.

Anyway, Danny became my best friend at school. We would get an upper classman to get us liquor and then we would take the vodka, meet at the commuter rail station with groceries and pour it into 6 pack bottles of Sprite so that it looked like we were bringing back groceries to the dorms. The security guard had no clue that we had 2 liters of vodka inside the bottles of soda and let us through. We got drunk to the point we passed out in our rooms. It was actually pretty pathetic. We had a lot of weekend nights where we would just get high, order Chinese food and lie in our beds listening to the Roots and A Tribe Called Quest. I loved listening to the Roots while I was high, it felt like I was on a journey; it felt amazing as if I was meditating and levitating while having a great bodily sensation. It felt so damn good. I miss those times. At the same time, as much fun we had with all the people we had met, I felt a loneliness inside. There was a void in my life; something was missing, and this chronic feeling of loneliness would continue to haunt me well into the present day. The fact was, Danny was very introverted and reserved, and was a good guy. That's what drew me to be his friend initially. However, I noticed as time went on, that he often acted weird and would talk to himself and withdraw from the world.

I remember Eminem's movie, *8 Mile*, and how much it meant to me. They had movie night at the Moakley Center and we all went to watch it. The thing is, Em had a rough life, and he inspired me so much because I felt like him. Nobody helped me financially, I felt unloved and uncared for. I was so fucking lost at Bridgewater, and that movie gave me the fuel that I needed to survive as well as care for myself. I'd go every day to run at the indoor track at the school's rec center. I loved hip hop and listened to powerful motivational music such as Eminem and Jay-Z, as well as 50 Cent and others. Their music was uplifting; it encouraged me to be the best I could be. I really enjoyed running. I'd put on my New Balances and head on down to the rec center where I'd run for a half hour. Running relieved my anxiety and stress; that's why I did it. It was soothing and helped me to clear my racing thoughts and worries. I felt at ease when I ran, it's a hobby that I'd continue to do for many years.

Freshman year was coming to an end and it was bittersweet to leave the school and all my friends behind; honestly, I was still not over Megan and what happened between us. I knew that she had apologized, but I couldn't stop thinking about her, and am first to admit that I was infatuated with her. I was desperately in need of help, so I sought advice from every person that I could, to the point where I knew that I was out of control. When I went home I even started sleeping with a woman who was married. Her name was Rebecca, and she was married to Dustin, who was schizophrenic, and a punk rock kind of guy who drank all day, talked about conspiracy theories and carried a big hunting knife on him. Dustin was paranoid. He would buy me liquor sometimes. Anyway, I was flirting a lot with his wife Rebecca, who also lived in my apartment complex. When freshman year was over, and I went back to Windsor Gardens for the summer, she invited me to her apartment and told me Dustin wasn't home. I went up to her apartment in my fancy playboy clothing from Express and with a fresh haircut without either considering how this would affect their marriage. I sat on the couch, and I remember that she scared me with a fake spider, I jumped up because it scared me. She laughed, and then proceeded to lick my face and glasses with her tongue. Then we went at it. We fucked on that couch. We were both extremely horny and just fucked each other's brains out. It was so good. She wanted me to come back at night another day but I never did. Then, things got ugly. Dustin found out that she had slept with me and beat Rebecca to a bloody pulp. The police were called, and he was arrested and went to jail for beating her. I felt so guilty. It was because I had slept with her that this all happened, and I vowed to never do it again-although you will come to find that I couldn't hold on to that promise.

I did what I did best to escape my problems—went to work. I had this mentality that money was the most important thing in the world, and that I had never had a silver spoon or anything ever handed out to you. I realized that in this world, nobody is going to give you anything and if you want something you must be the one to go out and get it.

Freshman year ended and I was working two fulltime jobs, I went back to Ocean State Job Lot to work with Spunge and Jose. I would get up early in the morning around 4am, and bike my ass through South Norwood, past Dean St to get to work there for 5am. They worked me hard, and after work finished at 1pm, I went on to my next job at the Dunkin Donuts on Rt 1 where I worked with some amazing Brazilian people. The thing is, I loved their work ethic. They worked 80 hrs a week, almost as much as me, if not more. I could relate to their struggle, after all, I AM the immigrant story. They motivated me; I worked so hard because of them starting at dawn and working well into the night, only to go to sleep and wake up the next morning to do it all over again.

From here on out in my story, I can warn you that things were getting worse for me. Spunge and Jose knew that I was working that much, and they wanted to take me out for a good time clubbing one night towards the end of summer. I worked early morning to late night, then woke up and did it all over again but at the time I didn't realize that I was full blown manic. I had endless energy with an undying hunger. On that one night when we had a guys' night out, Spunge drove us, and we are all having fun dancing until it was time to go home at 2am. I remember that on the way back I was drinking a big bottle of vodka in the car and was extremely inebriated. At one point, I rolled down the windows and attempted to throw the bottle of vodka out, only it didn't go out the window, instead, it hit the window and spilled all over Spunge and I. Spunge got understandably upset and went off on me, saying that "I was the stupidest person that he'd ever met." Now, after all I'd been through in high school with people teasing me that didn't sit well with me. I was really hurt by his words and my anger was building up. So we stopped the car and walk into the 711 in Walpole. That's when I exploded on Spunge. I yelled at him, saying something to the effect of, "you muthafucker I'll break your fucking nose! Who are you talking to like that!" Anyway, I scared the shit out of him; both him and Jose were visibly shaken by my fit of rage. I knew that I had scared them —hell, I scared myself. But the problem was that, as time went on, I didn't know how to control all this rage. So when they went back to the car, I told them that I'd walk home. They slowly drove away, and just like that they were gone, and I was alone walking 5 miles from the 7-11 in Walpole center on Route 1A to Windsor Gardens. I was walking in the rain, for 5 miles, afraid of myself and my inability to control my anger. I knew that I had just lost my best friends, and it really hurt. I remember it was like 3 am in the morning and

I was calling a mental health center trying to leave a voicemail to schedule an appt. There was something wrong with me. I was hurting people; what was worse that I had abused my best friends. I remember Jose telling me one day that Spunge is fragile, I'm a big guy and that someone my size could really hurt him so I needed to be careful. Anyway, I was going through emotional turmoil and was afraid of myself. I had just lost my two best friends, and everything went to shit from this moment on. I had a couple of weeks left working at Ocean State Job Lot before the summer came to an end, and Spunge avoided me. He averted his eyes when he walked past me and avoided me at all costs. I remember apologizing countless times to him, but he ignored me and wouldn't accept my apology. Jose also became distant, and the pain of losing them would haunt me for years to come. It was extremely difficult to forgive myself for my actions that caused me to lose my best friends. I had a problem with anger, and it was out of control.

SOPHOMORE SEMESTER @ BSC: LOSIN IT

I went back to Bridgewater for the start of sophomore year, but I was extremely burnt out. Something was off about me. I remember telling Derek about it; he tried to be sympathetic and told me that I was burnt out, and just needed to relax after all the work. I never got a break and relaxed, took a vacation, or anything. I needed to recharge the batteries. I remember taking a walk with Jenna and Megan and telling them about how my mental health was declining. I was paranoid of people judging me and always looking at me, and it was hard to walk through campus because I felt like people were all looking at me, staring at me in fact. I was anxious to even go to class and had terrible and overwhelming anxiety. I shared a dorm room at Miles Hall with Edison and some other weird guy named Jon who I disliked. He was just odd. Everything was fucked up. I chose to room with Edison because he was the cool, suave player, and now was a fraternity brother. Of course I wanted to fit in, but it was the wrong decision. Edison always had his frat brothers and women visiting our dorm, and I had terrible social anxiety. It happened so much that I had to go study at the library and just sit there at a desk because I was afraid of socializing with anyone.

I was afraid that they'd see my anxiety and would make fun of me for it, especially the women. One night, sitting in the library I scribbled a 2Pac quote on the desk that said, "No one knows my struggle, they only see the trouble, not knowing it's hard to carry on when no one loves you. Picture me inside the misery of poverty, no man alive has witnessed miracles that I survived." I love 2Pac, I was lost and troubled, and his music was the chicken soup for the soul that I needed. When I was manic in our dorm room I proclaimed myself as the "Hispanic 2pac." My roommates just laughed at me.

I went to see a psychiatrist in Brookline named Dr Heisel. He was a robust man who was sort of an asshole. My parents came once with me and told him that I expected financial help from them. He sided with them and told me that they were not responsible for me financially and that I was an adult. The good thing that came out of all this however, was that I was prescribed my first SSRI, known to the world as Zoloft. My father did try to help me. I'll never forget the day that he bought me a book called *The Feel Good Handbook* by David Burns. It was excellent, and I was surprised that he had bought me anything. The book really helped if you did the homework. The book stated that we all had distorted/negative forms of thinking, and it identified them. For example, one distorted thought pattern was jumping to conclusions, another was all or nothing thinking, when one thinks in terms of black and white with no in between. I definitely had that form of distorted thinking.

Back at my dorm with Edison and Jon, I made it clear that I had problems with my mental health. It was the anxiety and depression, and I was now taking Zoloft to combat them. I remember going to Sigma Chi frat parties that Edison and Charles invited me to, and I was extremely anxious and insecure. I followed Charles around like a lost puppy, and, if he went off even for a few minutes to go to the bathroom, I didn't know what to do with myself to relax. So I just left. I was becoming known as the guy who left parties without telling anyone. I hung out a lot in Danny's dorm room, or with Deron, an upper classmate who was half black and half Polish. I thought, how cool was that! Anyway, Deron was a good friend to me because he understood my problems and counseled me. I appreciated his help, but nothing seemed to help. I felt like I was out of control and losing my mind.

November came, classes were coming to an end and I was doing terribly academically. My school work had suffered and I was failing a few classes as well as getting C's in others. I remember one Thirsty Thursday night, Danny and I went to a Senior party in the apartments. The party was fun, and I remember drinking this red punch from a giant glass bowl. I drank and drank and drank, until I was absolutely obliterated. I remember talking to some girl from Brockton, and later other people asking me if I was okay. The rest of the night was a big blur. When I finally left the party with Danny, he went home and I went back to my dorm at Miles-Dinardo Hall. I passed out on my bed. A couple of hours later, I woke up to the sound of Edison opening the window and turning on a fan. The cold chill woke me up, and it smelled like shit. Hungover and half asleep, I asked Edison what was going on. He told me that I had shat myself. I hadn't even realized! I looked at my bed, and I was laying in shit. It was the most embarrassing thing that ever happened in my life. If I had been half asleep, I was now wide awake and panicking. Everyone knew. I couldn't hide it from anyone, not my roommates not my adjoining dorm roommates; Word spread fast and, before I knew it, the whole floor knew about my shitty night. Even Megan knew. I washed the sheets immediately and tried to save face. I could tell that my roommates felt bad because they knew that it was particularly embarrassing for me. After everyone went home for winter break, I remember my father driving over to pack up my things from my dorm. I was a mess, and I had decided Bridgewater State College for good. By the time that my roommates came back in January 2004, I wasn't there. I didn't even tell anyone that I was leaving. I just quietly picked up my things, left school and went home to my parents' apartment in Norwood. My father enrolled me in Bunker Hill Community College, in Charlestown. He said that it was a good school and told me to study there.

I immediately realized that I needed to change for the better, and so I joined the Rama Health Club and began working out hard. Me and my friend Dennis, who was also into weightlifting, would walk down the train tracks from Windsor Garden to South Norwood, where the Rama Health Club was. I wanted to change. I was keen to transform my body into something great. So I spent a lot of time on the elliptical as well as running laps around their mini indoor track. I also lifted weights and made sure I hit all the major muscle groups. I was seriously convinced that I was a U.S. Marine in my green Marine shirt. My work ethic in the gym was unparalleled. I worked out so hard. Of course, there were haters there, who laughed at me because I'd run the indoor track but fuck them, I stayed focused on me. Pretty soon, there was a weight loss contest that the gym offered. You basically had 8 weeks to shred as much fat as possible, and I wanted to win so badly I took this really seriously. I would workout 6 or sometimes 7 days a week and eat black beans with chicken for dinner. I ended up getting 2nd place and winning some money; it wasn't much but the most beautiful thing was seeing my name up there on the board for everyone to see. Number one went to this jackass who was extremely cocky and didn't like me. He was about two years older than I.

I loved going to the Rama and then going to take a nice hot shower with my Pure Sport Old Spice bodywash. That was the reward for my hard work. I remember one night when they were closing up the gym, they thought that everyone had left for the night, but I was still in the locker room taking a shower! So they locked me in! I went downstairs and panicked a little at first, but then I went to the cooler and grabbed a couple of cold Red Bulls for myself and filled up my duffel bag. Then I unlocked the door and left.

I absolutely loved it at Bunker Hill. First you had people from all walks of life, all different nationalities and ethnicities, and it was very diverse. I majored in Business Administration and took classes like Calculus I and Intro to Business, Communication, Computers, and accounting. I want the world to know that I hated calculus I and it took me three times to finally pass! I enjoyed meeting people in every class. I met one of my best friends there, a guy from Ghana named Justice; he helped me so much and looked after me to make sure I passed some of those challenging business courses. He ended up becoming Director of Student Central there. I'll never forget him he was a good guy.

When I was in school I was cocky and confident. I got the idea of buying things wholesale and then reselling to students. I bought TI-83 calculators wholesale on eBay and would purchase them for under $40 a calculator and resell for $80. The regular price was $120. I somehow believed that I was a genius "businessman/entrepreneur" and "marketer" and would make these advertisements to attract the college crowd so to sell the calculators, I created an ad with an image of a chubby kid with a t-shirt that said, "I fuck on the first date." Well, even though this was good for business, and people were enjoying the ad and calling me for the calculators, the administration at BHCC did not like it. They called my cell number and were pretty upset, saying that the picture of the chubby kid in the ad was one of their sons. I was so confused, so I went along with it. "That's your son?!" It confused them even more that I was confused, a sales tactic that I would learn to use. The more confused you are and ask questions when other people question you, the more information you would get out of them. Well, it worked, because they left me alone, but made me tear down the ads.

I really enjoyed how liberal Bunker Hill was. It was in Charlestown, a town rich and full of history. It was as lot of fun meeting the different types of people who were immigrants and were full of ambition. I enjoyed going to the computer lab and to the study halls in the D Lounge. I had a lot of fun. As much as I enjoyed going to the classes the first semester, I was still highly manic throughout the term, since I hadn't yet been diagnosed with Bipolar Disorder. I began thinking that school was a waste of time again. Instead of paying for classes which could be thousands of dollars each semester (even though the community college was very affordable back then), I could be out hustling hard, and working two jobs while saving every penny I could. So that's exactly what I did. In May of 2004 when classes were wrapping up for the term I left Bunker Hill so that I could get to work. It's important to note that during this time my parents moved to rent the first floor of a house at 64 Sanborn Ave in West Roxbury. The very first job that I got, was at Boch Honda from 7 am in the morning to 3 pm, then I'd go down to Home Depot and work until 1 in the morning. I'd like to speak about my work history a little bit because it ties it in perfectly with my mental health history and how someone who has bipolar and anxiety functions at work.

My first job was as a lot attendant for Boch Honda in Norwood on the Auto Mile. I enjoyed the work because I got to drive the best cars—not just Hondas, I'm talking about the trade-ins. My favorite car that I got to drive was the Lexus LS460. I swear it was the most comfortable ride that I had ever driven. Another great car to drive was the Acura MDX, smooth as butter! You have to understand that I wasn't accustomed to driving such great cars, so I drove it down during my break to our apartment complex in Windsor Gardens, and my brother and a couple of friends got in and drove around. Here's where it got ugly. I had been suffering from severe anxiety and panic attacks because George, my supervisor, was extremely verbally abusive. He was a spiteful Greek man who would yell at you for everything, and everyone knew he was nuts. Often times he just wanted to look good in front of the ladies that worked there. He humiliated me every day, and when it came time to actually do things like park cars in a straight line, or parallel park them, he would yell and put pressure on me, and hence I fucked up more cars at Boch than anyone in the history of working there! I'd scratch them and dent them by crashing into other cars. The anxiety had such a strong hold over me that I literally let it control me. I'd arrive to work a nervous wreck. I sometimes drove the company van from the parking lot at Sal and Vinnie's to Boch Honda/Toyota to get the salespeople to work. Again, social anxiety is defined as feeling people are making an intense judgement about you. You feel that everyone is staring at you or talking about you, and when I had 8 passengers it made me extremely nervous. One time, I took a left turn into the Boch Honda lot, but, as I was turning everyone got scared and yelled in panic because they thought that I turned too soon and almost hit a car. It was really embarrassing for me that I was viewed as a nervous wreck who couldn't do anything right. I wasn't competent. I was weak. It was hard to be myself around people. I was even made fun of because I drove a piece of shit hooptie—it was a white 1992

Toyota Corolla with a bad muffler that meant it made a really loud noise. As if that wasn't enough, the car had a painted-on blue driver side door that I had done myself with a bottle of spray paint because I had thought that it would look good-I was wrong. Eventually one of the grease monkeys at the shop offered to replace the exhaust manifold for my Toyota for $150. The worst thing I ever did, was when I was going home early one day and I went to the employee parking lot at Sal and Vinnies only to find that my car had been blocked in by other cars. This didn't stop me; I don't know what I was thinking but I remember I drove into the other car with my foot down on the gas and pushed the car over so that I could get my car out. I damaged a couple of cars pretty badly and I honestly did feel bad, but I felt more afraid of getting caught. But don't tell Mr. Boch; let's keep that our little secret. I honestly think that Boch knew about me damaging all those cars, he just let it slide because he felt sorry for me. Plus, my supervisor George was an asshole. It's funny how people who don't break the cycle of abuse see victims of abuse and think of them as weak and continue the abuse. George was a son of a bitch. He'd publicly humiliate me and yell at me all the time. I felt like shit, and the worst part was that I took it from him. He wasn't a nice man at all...

    I had a lot of balls back then. I remember the Funkmaster Flex Celebrity Car Show in 2003 held at the Bayside Expo Center. This was great because we got to meet a lot of celebrities-I met Jim Jones, Juelz Santana, Sean Paul, and Lil Kim. But what I really wanted was a picture with me and Funkmaster Flex. When I saw him, he brushed me off and said he'd do it later. I was upset. So I made a point of finding him later. After the show, I saw Funk Flex with his team on the opposite side of the traffic flow to. I was so keen to get my picture with him, I drove on the opposite side of traffic going fast. Cars were honking at me all the way; thank God that there were no police cars there otherwise I could easily have been arrested. As I approached FMF and his team, you could tell he was a little scared. But anyway, I pulled up, asked him for a picture with my one time use flash camera (remember those?). He rejected me again, so I replied "but you told me earlier that I could take a picture with you." Then he succumbed and agreed to do it. My friend Matty had my camera; when he tried to click the button to take the picture, the film had ran out! I was so pissed. But instead, I had FMF sign the hood of my white Corolla, which looked amazing. I talked to him for about a minute, and asked him if he liked my car, told him that the muffler was broken, and he said "that's alright." I felt that real recognizes real, and in our case he saw that I had come for what I wanted and was going to stop at nothing to get it. And Flex respected that. We gave each other daps and left. That was my Funk Master Flex story (Drop bomb here).

My other job was at Home Depot, where I didn't like it one bit. They put me in Kitchen and Bath, threw me on the sales floor and expected me to help people buy toilets when I had no knowledge of how to install them or anything! I was told by one of the army vets there that I lacked, "intestinal fortitude." But I'd slack off as much as possible there. It was heavy labor work, for example using one of those machines to lift me up and put those heavy ass toilets onto the shelves. I remember sometimes I would nap on one of the shelves near the insulation for a few minutes, where no one could find me. They really worked me over there, it was ridiculous.

At Boch Honda, everything came to an end when the Vice President's daughter came to work for the summer and I decided to hang out with her and take her to lunch. I don't know why, I probably misread her signals, but I attempted to kiss her. She did not take kindly to that, and told HR. They fired me instantly. When these stupid things happen, it's important not to dwell on them and take them too seriously (for god's sake I was like 18 at the time) but what is important is to always learn from your mistakes. Don't dwell on what happened, instead keep moving to achieve your goal. At that time, my goal was to hold two full time jobs to save money to buy a Subway Franchise, so I was immediately proactive and drove up and down the Auto mile applying for jobs at dealerships.

My next morning job was at the Hyundai on the Auto mile. I'll be honest, I didn't like it one bit there. It was boring and nobody talked to me. I was in the service department. There was this one hick that was a total asshole to me; once he got mad cause I accidentally looked over his shoulder while he was typing an email. He was a loser. Another mechanic, a Latino, ironically, kind of bullied me around, saying this wasn't a job for me, and that I belonged in an office. The worst of it came when I had to park a Chevy Silverado into the bay and, as I was pulling into it backwards, I scratched it on the side. The customer was pissed but I apologized profusely. I felt terrible, and it seemed that everyone had seen it, so I got fired from that job.

Next, I drove to the HR office of the Gallery Group, a better place to work than Boch enterprises or Hyundai. I walked in, asked to speak to the HR lady and was greeted by Grace Law. I basically charmed her and told her that I was looking for a fulltime job, I was a hard worker and would be a great asset to her team. The next day I was hired and training at the Mazda Gallery. After about a week, I was transferred over to the Volkswagen Gallery, on Providence Highway. I started out as a cashier and continued to work hard. I had the greatest boss, Bob Hershman, who was the general manager. He knew that I was timid and had tremendous anxiety around the customers, but he told me that I needed to expose myself and face people, and that the more I did it the more it, the better I'd get at it as well as becoming more comfortable. What I didn't like was long lines; one time, I had a panic attack because of the long line, and Mr. Herschman had to come in and save me. I remember telling a customer, "Wow I thought I was gonna die." He replied that it wasn't normal to feel that way. I really enjoyed that job, I got to drive customers home as well as pick them up, and work with the sales team which I loved. Eventually I got promoted by Bob to Customer Service representative in the service department. I really enjoyed that job and the fact that I had my own office. This was one of my favorite jobs and it's important to note this because it was one of the few jobs where I didn't get fired but excelled instead. I was good at it and I loved working there.

Home Depot didn't end well for me. I got fired when I was outside with a forklift and accidentally ran over a tarp; it took the workers almost an hour to get it untangled from the base of the forklift. When Jordan, the Assistant Manager of Home Depot saw that, he immediately called me into his office, and fired me. I felt bad, but I didn't let it stop me. I had resilience, so onward and upward, I thought, and I continued marching forward. The next afternoon job I got was at BJ's Wholesale Club in Dedham.

2004 Bunker Hill

I meet some cool friends at Bunker Hill. I hung out with Christian, Brian, and James. We planned to go to Miami for spring break but at the last-minute Christian couldn't make it, so it was just me and Brian. Brian seemed loyal, and so I trusted him. In fact, his mother didn't wire him the money that he said that he needed so I ended up covering him for about $300 on our trip. One night, we went to a club, and these older women started taking an interest in Brian. There was a white lady who was married, and her friend, this Asian woman in white pants which were see through, so you could see a nice thong on her. Anyway, they were in a VIP booth, and invited us to join them. They obviously had money. I wanted both of them, especially the Asian girl. I danced with her while Brian danced with the white lady. But eventually, when I tried to kiss the Asian girl, she rejected me. I didn't ALWAYS end up getting the girl. There were times when I didn't, and it hurts to not be wanted. After all, everyone's desire is to be desired. Anyway, they wanted Brian, and so I just took advantage of the fact that the ladies purchased a big bottle of vodka and orange juice and kept drinking it. Eventually, Brian didn't want to take the women home, so we left their little VIP booth and continued clubbing.

The trip was fun, but the problem came at the end, when Brian owed me $300 and didn't pay me back. As a matter of fact, he never paid me back, and later disappeared from my life. That bothered me. He wasn't a true friend.

I don't say a lot of good things about my father because I never forgave him for the way he treated me growing up, but I do have to say that in some aspect I idolized the man. Yes, he was eccentric and impulsive and had a temper, but when he wanted to, he could be the coolest guy. For instance, I purchased a used cell phone in Chelsea, which ended up being defective. The receipt clearly said no refunds, and the owner at the counter spoke Spanish so it was hard to talk to him about returning the phone. One day, my father went into the phone store with me, and there were other customers who witnessed this miracle as well. He walked up to the guy and in Spanish he started persuading him to accept my phone. He ended up using the customers and incorporating them into his sales pitch. He was charming, funny, and manipulative to the point where the guy who didn't want to accept it back, actually took the phone back and refunded me my money. I looked at my father at that moment as if he was my hero, because deep down he was. I had a love/hate relationship with him, but he could be great. He was great—its just that his demons got the best of him at times. But that was one day that I was truly proud that he was my father.

VW GALLERY AND BJS

VW Gallery and BJs were the jobs where I was probably happiest while working. I loved VW Gallery because I felt good about what I did—customer service—and then at BJs I was a recovery specialist. This was great because they gave me a walkie-talkie while I stocked product, milk, and consolidated product and put the empty boxes into a box bin. But my main job was helping customers find products and helping with mattresses and tires. It was a highly active job, and I was in excellent shape! Everything was going great—I was being recognized for my work and there was talk about me becoming a manager. But it never happened. I was hypomanic a lot of the time, I recall one day when I pretended to be a manager and I gave the customer a discount on an item. When management found out about that, they called me in and gave me an ultimatum, basically telling me that I couldn't go around impersonating being a manager. BJ's was cool though. We had a Christmas Party, I enjoyed that; it felt like a big family, or a big community of people who had your back. I met a lot of young people like me there. There was this older woman who was probably around 39 when I was only 22. She was a total MILF. Her name was Kathy. I'll never forget her because she would always flirt with me. One day, she wanted to show me her implants, and took me to the bathroom where she unbuttoned her shirt, undid her bra and let me feel her tits. I was so on cloud nine. I thought this was a dream, but when I proceeded to kissing her neck she laughed and pushed me gently away. She was a total tease. But to this day, I get a chubby just thinking about her. Her mouth, her voice, and her big breasts. She was a bad girl., and I'll never forget her.

Everything started going sour when a beautiful 19 year old girl name Reama came to work for the summer. Reama was Lebanese, and she was absolutely gorgeous. She had these hypnotizing green eyes, and a smile that just melted me, I really liked her. She began flirting with me and I immediately developed a huge crush on her. All the guys talked about her including me and this other kid named John. John was sure that he was going to win her, so I had some competition. Things turned for the worse as I saw Reama more and more with John and not me. One day, I even saw her with him in his car. I was livid, feeling that she had led me on, but more importantly I was losing the battle with John. I hated him, but more importantly, now I started resenting Reama, who was just a tease. It'd also got really ugly when my friend Sean was walking and talking to Reama and they walked past me. I got anxiety along with an uncontrollable rage and resentment. The problem wasn't that it wasn't okay to be angry, but the fact that I still wore my emotions on my sleeve and that my face looked red and full of rage, as if I was about to explode at any minute. They saw this, and later when I spoke to Sean he told me that it had made them uncomfortable. I didn't know what to do. I asked everyone and even the customers for advice about her. It was a difficult time for me and my mental health was descending quickly. So I called the BJs Employee Assistance Program, told the intake lady what was going on, and what happened next was great. She hooked me up with a social worker name Martin Zafran, who practiced near my home in West Roxbury. Marty was probably one of the best therapists I ever had. He would work with me on correcting my anger problems by changing the way that I thought. VW Gallery and BJ's was difficult to work at, especially with this girl problem, but I handled it as best as I could, because at the time I was a runner, running 6 days a week. This helped me improve my anxiety tremendously.

Another thing that happened in 2004 was that Pablo graduated Norwood High, and was on his way to Mass Maritime Academy, a military school in Buzzards Bay, MA Cape Cod. I was very proud of my him—he not only was my best friend, but he inspired me to be better. The first few years I would drive him to school from West Roxbury every weekend. I'm not sure if he remembers that but it took a lot of hard work and sacrifice to get him to be successful at school. He had it extremely difficult there—at the beginning, he was taunted and teased a lot, and the rich privileged white kids were very racist towards him, but he was strong. He later told me that when he felt like giving up, he thought of me, and that motivated him to finish strong. I teared up when I heard that.

I loved my brother but living in West Roxbury we were leading two different lives, and it's hard to intervene into someone's life to tell them that they're not doing the right thing or even just to offer advice or their support. I was on one path and my brother was on his path in military school. Between my jobs I rarely got to see him. But when we were home, I was jealous of him. I was a loner, who ran to subside my strong emotions of pain and anger and whatever else. Sometimes when I ran, I cried thinking about things. And he was popular during his college years. Maybe it was because he always had the Russians come over to see him, and I had nobody. There were times where we shared a twelve pack by the commuter rail in West Roxbury, but other times, I went to the liquor store and bought a pint of Captain Morgan rum then drove up and down Route 1, drinking in the car. I was hurting inside, and wanted someone, anyone to help me. I remember going into the drive through at Taco Bell and ordering my food, then asking the kid at the window to throw away my empty bottle of rum. As you can imagine the teen at the counter took my bottle and was shocked that I had just handed him an empty bottle of rum. Other times I'd be drunk and abuse our hamster. I took him, threw up on him and threw him in the bathtub. Then I started crying because I thought I might have broken his leg. My mother told me "you can't do that it's a harmless pet", and I began to cry.

Another time I remember that my family was out of the state and I was depressed. Not only did I drink 13 Bud Light beers, I also ordered two large cheese pizzas from Denos and binge ate them. Then my brother and his friend Sergei walked into the house and saw me, drunk and pathetic eating two boxes of cheese pizza. My brother normally didn't know how to deal with me when I was sad, depressed or in a manic state, but Sergei said that it was sad to see me like this. I'll never forget that.

But the worst of it was when our neighbor, Mr. Carvajal, aka "un vecino" from Harlem died. He had heavy surgery on his back and with the strong medication that he was taking, he drank heavily and died in his sleep. We were going to his funeral in New York City as a family. My father was driving, when all of a sudden I saw one of those Red Bull marketing vans, and so I opened my door while we were in moving traffic to ask for a sample, and my father yelled for me to get back inside the car. My brother did something that made me extremely angry. He said "sit down you idiot!" and proceeded to slap my head. Then my father told him to leave me alone and told him that I was sick. The anger in me festered and grew until

I couldn't hold it any longer. My own little brother putting me in my place like that, and it made me see the reality of how my father thought of me—he was pitying me for being sick. When we arrived at the funeral home I began crying and yelling and swinging punches at my brother. My brother (who knew how to fight by the way) dodged my punches and didn't hit me back, he just basically kept dodging my punches while I was chasing him all over the parking lot of the funeral home. My father said to me, "Look at how people are looking at you," referring to other people who were staring in disbelief at my lashing out at my brother. I was really hurt, but as time passed it healed my wound. They didn't respect me because they didn't understand me. It was that fucking simple. They didn't know how to help me… Hell, how could they—I didn't know how to help myself.

Back to the VW Gallery. I clicked really well, especially with the sales managers and the sales guys. You see, I was a sales guy at heart, but never had the heart to apply and become a salesman for VW. But one of the people there who was incredibly interesting was Luis Rezendes, the used car sales manager. He was a smooth, suave, charming Cape Verdean young guy who was very easy to talk to. He always had a positive mentality and warmed up to people easily. He was always trying to talk me into going into sales and saying that I'd be great at it.

I became Bob Herschman's (the General Manager) favorite worker, so once I got promoted to Customer Service Rep I worked more on the service side. One day, Bob had asked me to play good music for him on his audio system for the dealership to hear. I made him a custom playlist, mainly of feelgood music such as The Killers and other rock and roll that was appropriate for the clientele. One day however, I accidentally turned up the volume too high and the speakers were about to burst they were so loud! Bob yelled angrily and came to see what was going on. This was not good, but when I looked up at him and apologized, all embarrassed, he instantly forgave me.

In the summer of 2005 I met a pretty blonde girl from Walpole named Meggy. I met her while I was checking her car out. She was into me, so I got her number. We began having a fling, she wanted me to drive down to Union College where she went to school and I would drive three hours to upstate New York and bring her flowers, just to spend the night having sex. We were both really horny, and my parents let her spend the night in their West Roxbury home on Sanborn Ave once, so that I could get laid. We were like two jack rabbits. The worst part of it was, that after that evening, they would never allow her to spend the night because my father (being the strong Catholic man that he was) felt me having sex with her in his home was disrespectful to him. How? I have no idea, but she wasn't allowed. So, we did what any other two young lovers would do—we'd have sex in public places, like restaurants and I remember one time the Kohl's Dressing room at the Walpole Mall. We fucked in her VW Beetle, in the backseat, can you imagine how much thinner and in shape I must have been to be able to smash in that small car? We'd do it a lot, and then for a week my parents left to California with my brother Pablo, so I had the house all to myself. I had Meggy spend the night for the whole week and we just had sex. Our relationship ended not long after her mother (who I disliked) told me not to have sex in their home. Well, I broke the rules and fucked Meggy upstairs, then her mother kicked me out and told me to never to come back to their home again.

I remember one time she invited me some to guy's party in Walpole. . My brother came along with us and Meggy's friend wanted me to buy her beer. I bought her some Bud Light , and then at the party, I asked the girl to pay me back. Well, as she was about to hand me the money, she started giving me an attitude, and I didn't understand what the problem was. She knew that she had to pay me back but she didn't want to?! It didn't make sense. So anyway, as she was about to hand me the money, this guy came from out of nowhere, and interrupted her and said to her, "keep your money." And then he told me that she wasn't gonna pay me back the money. I was shocked to hear this from this fat boy. I got into an angry shouting match with him, and he pulled a knife out on me. Someone else pulled another knife on me... I didn't see that one coming! Anyway, my brother pulled me away and as he was pulling me away, he said that he never felt me being so strong and angry as I tried to get away from my brother's hold and beat the shit out of the fat hillbilly. As I was being taken away all I heard was, "Get him out of here" That just made me angrier. I got into the car and was furious. I ended up breaking up with Meggy that night. The reason was she stood by her friend and was defending her instead of me! It was just a fling it didn't even last three months. I thanked Pablo for his help afterward.

I lasted at the VW Gallery for two years; I was very proud of this because I had previously developed this feeling that I was never good enough for a job due to me getting fired so frequently. But I felt that I had to go back and finish school. So I left at the end of 2005 as I prepared to finish up my Associates degree in Business and transfer that fall to Northeastern's Bachelors of Science Leadership program. It was night school and I was embarking on a whole new adventure!

As I said, in 2005 I made a few friends at Bunker Hill, like Christian, Brian, and James. Justice was probably my best friend there.

He looked out for me. I did stupid things, like go drinking Heineken in Boston Common with James on a Friday night, and then go back to Bunker Hill where he left his car in the parking lot—only it was blocked by a police car. I drove up to the police car and saw the officer napping and I didn't want to wake him, so I drove past him and into the parking lot, and James got into his car. Then the police pulled me over. He was pissed and asked why I passed him when there was a clear sign saying do not enter. I just told him that he had been sleeping and I hadn't wanted to wake him. There was nothing he could say; the officer wasn't supposed to be sleeping on duty, but he acted like he was gonna do something anyway. He took my ID and said that he was going to speak to the Dean about me. Then we left; I learned my lesson that night-always wake up sleeping officers on the job, and then ask if you may enter!

I was just working at BJ's and at Bunker Hill finishing up my associates degree, when I did something I should never have done. You see, BJ's was a community of people; it felt like family, and we would do things for each other. For example, I'd get the deli department cans of Red Bull and other shit and they'd hook me up with chicken tenders. During this time I definitely felt like I had a case of kleptomania. So I had a bin that I rolled around filled with boxes. I'd take whatever I wanted—anything from DVDs, music, cologne and Red Bull energy drink, LOTS of Red Bull. I'd take them to the milk cooler where I'd go inside and use my box-cutter to cut through the security tags and cut out the actual movie or perfume, and then dump the box that the cologne or movie was in and mix it in with the boxes, then throw them in a trash can behind the cooler where there were no cameras. I was extremely slick but overly confident, thinking that I could never get caught. Boy was I wrong! The manager Brian had set up a hidden surveillance camera in the back loading dock to see who the thief was. They put out cases of opened Red Bulls and sure enough, I walked right into the trap and drank and enjoyed the Red Bull. The next day, Brian called me into the Office, where he was accompanied by Josh, the Loss Prevention guy. Brian told me that they had caught me stealing Red Bull and gave me a talk that made me feel extremely guilty of. He said that how could I do this to him, to BJ's, after all the talks that he'd had with me about a career at BJs and my fear of public speaking. He told me that he wasn't going to call Dedham Police to have them take me out in handcuffs (normally that's what they did; even my friend Sean was escorted that way) but told me that I was fired, and that he never wanted to see me in this store again. I felt like shit for a while. I felt like I had let him down, and let a whole community of people down. The worst part was, I had truly enjoyed working there; it kept me active and busy and the job was a great fit for me. I'll never forget BJ's and to this day I remember the lesson I learned and do not touch anything that doesn't belong to me.

I was lonely in West Roxbury, and although I did have friends from Bunker Hill, living at home with my father around wasn't easy at all. It was extremely difficult to deal with him. I couldn't even go into the kitchen for a late-night snack because he'd wake up and yell at me because apparently, I made noise doing it. My whole life felt as if I was walking on eggshells with him around, and it was extremely hard. But I had no choice. I was enrolled in Bunker Hill and worked mainly as an escape so I didn't have to deal with him or try to fill the void of loneliness. My father would still act irrationally with me all the time, we'd get into arguments where he called the Boston Police on me. Do you know how embarrassing that was? To have two of Boston's Finest come to our house and try to explain to me the important of moving out at an early age. They didn't understand my situation... my father should have been smarter than that. When he called them, he told them that "my son is bipolar." That really hurt my feelings, but I was able to keep calm and they finally left. I had no respect for him.

Sometimes my parents would leave, I remember one Christmas they left me home alone for both Christmas Eve and Christmas Day. I was home alone, and lonely. I felt abandoned and neglected. I've always hated my father for the way that he puts himself and his needs first, and doesn't care about anyone else, while my mother was too afraid of him to put her foot down and followed him around like a lost puppy. I remember one day my father took us to Washington DC for Christmas. He's the type of guy who doesn't like family gatherings or waiting for anything. He's extremely restless, and impatient. We reached a hotel, where we were staying, and for Christmas day we walked around DC. I was upset that there was no tree, no presents—no Christmas spirit whatsoever. My father firmly believed that the presents were only for little kids, and by this point we were teenagers. This was when I was only 12. From then on there was no more Christmas.

My brother sometimes came home to Westy for the weekend and vacations, and we would go out Friday nights and buy a beer and just talk. He received a lot of demerits for either fighting or talking back to upper classmen. They tried to get him to quit, but still, he never did. I love my brother more than anything because he is a living extension of me, and we were so close.

2006 Northeastern University

I loved living in West Roxbury. In 2006 I started classes at Northeastern Evening school. The major was leadership and, as I walked into a room full of older adults, I felt immediate anxiety. Everyone was at least 20 to 30 years older than me in this program. I instantly clicked with the minorities—the first girl I met was a Haitian named Myrlande and we became friends. Then there was her friend, Medgine, who was a beautiful Haitian girl who nobody seemed to like because of her stuck up attitude. There was also Jose, who was from Columbia, and was also one of my first friends there. Everybody pretended to be welcoming at first, but they excluded Medgine. At the time I was working at the Harvard Medical School Admissions Office (how many people get to do that!) thanks mainly to my mother, who worked in the school's HR Dept and hooked me up. This was a temporary position lasting six months, but I worked as an Admissions Coordinator, and I had to sort mail, file, scan applications and recommendation letters as well. I worked with Jason Graff, a writer, and Ivan, who was from Russia and was a cynical man. The goal was to obtain a permanent position as a Staff Assistant at Harvard, and my mother was trying to help me to do that. But honestly, I wasn't being true to myself, I hated being in the office, although the people were fun. I had a terrible time with my

ADHD and was known to do pushups in the Harvard Medical School Admissions Office while accepting only the finest medical students in the world. I was lucky to have this job. The problem came when I asked the assistant Director Paul, to put in a good word for me to get a permanent job here. He said sure he would, only he did the exact opposite. He told Linda Picard, the HR lady at HMS who worked alongside my mom that he didn't think the positions here at Harvard would be a good fit for me, and that I seemed bored. I was furious at him, and went to talk to Joanne, the Director of Admissions. I told her that Paul was supposed to give me a good recommendation and instead he had totally butchered my chances of ever getting a permanent job at the medical school. Nothing came out of it, what was done was done, and by April 2007, I had left Harvard Medical School.

There were a few good things that happened. Number one, I banged Medgine, the pretty Haitian girl, and then I banged her again at her place in Hyde Park. I stood up for Medgine when she decided to leave the program after the first semester. I was saying that she left because the cohort didn't include her but others disagreed.

Things got worse for me at Northeastern. As I mentioned before, I had ADHD, and had a hard time sitting still, and was pretty impulsive and all that good stuff. On Saturdays, my classes were six hours long, and often I left class early. People didn't take too kindly to that. Eventually something happened where I wasn't picked for a team and did the assignment by myself due to me being absent and we got onto this long argument with a stupid classmate on Blackboard, an online communication tool, where she said that it was my own fault people perceived me the way that they do. I came across as unreliable and not dependable because I'd leave classes early.

I had to explain that I had ADHD, that this was known as protected health information, and I didn't have to share anything about my disability with her. However, someone who really helped me with rebutting to that evil woman's message to me was my new girlfriend, Anette.

I had met her when I signed up for Match.com dating online. She was a poet, good with words, and wicked smart and I fell for her instantly. Anyway, more on how we met later, but I just want the world to know that Anette (who I called Anet) helped me write this beautiful letter about my disability. It shed a lot of light on how people were ignorant to the ways of someone who had learning difficulties and how they behaved, but more importantly, how the cohort had reacted to the way that I behaved. They thought I was just being a jackass by leaving early, but the reality of it was that I had a learning disorder; couldn't pay much attention and couldn't sit still, so after about four hours of sitting, I bounced, because I couldn't stand sitting any longer.

ANETTE 2006

Our first date was at the Starbucks in West Roxbury. I was a nervous wreck. She was into me though, so we started talking more and I began hanging out in her apartment in her parent's two-family house down in Roslindale. She had the top floor of the house, and I felt so free and at ease being with her. I was heavily drinking, and every time I came over to her apartment I would buy Belvedere Vodka or Sizzurp and drink. Then we'd fuck, and we had rough sex. Anette was short, curvy and chubby, and I loved hitting it from behind. I loved watching her moan and enjoy my cock. It was real good at first. So what happened? I tend to develop this pattern where I meet the girl then move in with her to avoid living with my father—sooo, I did just that. I moved in with Anette at first and we lived there for a bit. We had a lot of fun; she read me award-winning poetry and invited me to a party for her graduate school, Boston University, where I got to see Bob Dylan's childhood bathtub in her professor's office of all places. It was hard to mingle with any of her friends. one of her friends noticed my behavior and said, aww he's so shy! Anyway, the point is, we went places together such as Charleston, South Carolina to visit her friend Joanne. We partied, we had a lot of fun, we went to Faneuill Hall to Ned Devine's and other pubs. I'll talk more about her later.

NEU

During my time at Northeastern, I wanted to party as much as I could since I was young and fertile. I met a friend named Jay Stack, at a security job for Allied Barton in Cambridge at the Biogen location. Stack also went to Northeastern; he was majoring in criminal justice and he wanted to be a cop. He had been in a severe coma that almost cost him his life, but luckily he recovered and continued to drink and party with me. He introduced me to a beautiful Irish lass named Jen, and I also met my good friend Rodney at the Biogen security in Cambridge. We all worked together, and we began partying a lot together. We would go out frequently to places such as The Purple Shamrock in Faneuill Hall or the Liquor Store, which was a club with a mechanical horse that you could ride. During this time I drove drunk much more than I should have. I remember driving to Faneuill Hall, parking somewhere on Stafford St, and walking to the bars. We'd meet girls, make out with random ones and have a lot of fun, but when last call came, and it was 2am, I'd drive home drunk, once crashing into the bushes at the VFW Parkway Rotary in West Roxbury on my way home. Another time I went to Lil Peach, the convenience store on the corner of Spring St and Temple St. I was hammered, and as I pulled in I didn't brake hard enough and the kid that was just standing there in the way got tapped by my car. I didn't care, I was obliterated.

Other times after the bars I'd walk with Stack on Mass Ave to go to his apartment on Columbus Ave. He happened to live in the prestigious Douglas Ave apartments. We'd get a slice of pizza; he was the first person to introduce me to *Entourage*, a great series on HBO. We'd have a lot of fun, and he became one of my best friends during that time. Another time we were hammered walking down Mass Ave to Columbus Ave when I heard loud hip hop. That's right, someone was throwing a party. I told Stack to sneak in through the window with me. So that's how we got in. We danced we had fun, and after the party went home. One time I was lost somewhere in Roxbury off of Columbus Ave, and these Puerto Ricans were circling around me and were gonna rob me but then I started speaking Spanish to them, and they embraced me. Culture is everything to me, especially my Latino culture. It is my ethnicity and culture that can take a complete stranger and build a bond with them. It's a beautiful thing. One time I went up drunk and to some projects in Roxbury to help a drunk man get to his room. I took him up the elevator and got him to his apartment. When I came down, another elderly black man looked at me and said, "What are you doing here? Why are you here? You don't belong here!" I was hurt but also drunk, so I started thinking about what that man said. Why was I there? Narrowly speaking, because I wanted to help the drunk elderly man find his way home, but at the same time, I knew I was trying to find my way, not only home, but in the world.

Stack, Jen and I went to Oktoberfest and had a lot of fun meeting new people and getting drunk and dancing. That was a good time.

I was getting more comfortable with myself and I had decided that the secret was alcohol! One day we ran into an old classmate from Norwood High Sean Murphy, at Senor Frogs in Boston. Me and Stack were partying, when Sean saw me dancing with two girls. He looked at me and just laughed. He couldn't believe that the shy and socially awkward kid from high school was now on the dance floor dancing with some girls. We spoke for a bit, and I ended up telling him that high school had been a really bad time for me; it had been when I was being physically abused by my father, and I was fucked up. I guess he felt bad, because when he threw a party and I found out he lived in Mission Hill, I took my brother and we went to the party. Most people were cool, some were not too thrilled to see me. But I was just happy that Sean did something as nice as to invite me to one of his parties. I have nothing but good things to say about Sean. He is a good standup guy, and I'll forever remember his good character and his integrity.

Another time we decided to throw a party at Stack's apartment. We got two Bud Light Ball kegs and invited a bunch of people, but few came. I remember my brother coming to that one and we both got extremely wasted playing Beer Pong. My brother eventually passed out on top of a dresser and I got locked out somehow and kept knocking on Stack's door but he didn't let me in. That pissed me off. I began to walk around drunk off my ass and opening random people's doors and entering their apartments and grabbing more beers out of the fridge. Then, I damaged some property when I started punching the surveillance cameras and knocking them from the walls and breaking them. I did all this, and still no one ever caught me. Maybe I wanted to be caught, so someone could finally say "enough is enough" and get me the help I need. I was destructive and often didn't know how to handle myself when I got this way—and it got much worse when I drank. Stack was a privileged white kid from Poughkeepsie New York, whose father had bought him a red Corvette after he came out of that coma. His friends and family were from Long Island; they were very snobby and arrogant. But anyway, I was determined to get back into the apartment, so I pulled the fire alarm, and that woke everyone up for sure! Stack was mad at me for doing that, but I had to get in, and once I got in, I ran to get my brother, who I found sleeping on top of a dresser, Snoopy-style. How he got up there beats me. I woke him eventually even though it took over 10 minutes, and he got up and we went outside while the fire department came and checked out the building.

Eventually Stack left the security job and I followed him. I didn't need it, and I quit right after he did. Rodney was also one of my best friends back in the day; he even met Anette at one point, but he got mad at me after I sold him a pair of tickets to see Jay-Z in concert at the Garden because I told him that he'd be sitting so close to Jay-Z that he could see his nose hairs! Instead, he found out when he got there that that was far from the truth, and he was sitting way up high in the nosebleeds far away from the stage. He didn't want to pay me, and so again, I lost my temper and went off at him on the phone. He never did pay me for those tickets, but what was worse was that I lost a good friend that day... sometime in 2009 I believe. It wouldn't be until more than a decade later that me and Rodney would reconnect but more on that later.

Brookline

Meanwhile, things were looking good with Anette and I, and so we ended up moving into a studio in Brookline on Carlton St. I was really happy with my life. I had left Harvard and started as an Inside Sales Representative at a lead generation company. My job was to use fake aliases and convince Fortune 500 company CEO's and other executives of the company to schedule an introductory meeting with one of my clients. I pitched network security, virtualization and shit like that but I had no idea what these things were. My job was just to convince the execs of those Fortune500 companies that my clients had the best tech products and they needed to meet with them!

When I first got to the job, I met with Harry Guzpacho, the HR hiring manager. He was a pudgy short creepy looking guy, but he was nice to me. He was the one who hired me and asked if I could read a script and dial a phone 150 plus times a day. For what they were paying me, of course I could! I had a base salary of $35k plus my commissions were set at $50 per meeting set; on average I was doing 30-40 meetings a month. You do the math. I loved it!

They put me with the new training team for my first month, where I had the most set meetings that month, I got 25. They awarded me a plaque at our next team luncheon meeting, and

I couldn't have been prouder of myself. After a month, they told me that I'd go to another team, the Mustangs. When I first arrived there, I met with Chris, the team manager. He seemed nice, but I found later that he favored certain people and was two-faced. He only had the job because he was dating or married to the owner's daughter.

At at the beginning I was extremely insecure being on the team. After that, I had 37 meetings that first month with my new team! They loved me, but only because I was setting a lot of meetings for the team-I was on fire! I remember one of my coworkers we'll call him Submit, would talk to me a lot to try to find out what I was doing. He said that he usually set a lot of meetings the way I did, but this month wasn't doing too good. Submit was a real douchebag, he was annoying, and seemed to have a really bad case of ADHD. He talked obnoxiously, was loud, and most important to note, was jealous of me because I was the new guy and was off to an excellent, start, setting almost 40 meetings that first month. The goal was, to try to get 100 meetings in 90 days. If you did that they bumped up your base pay to $50k a year, and for each meeting you set after that they paid you $100. I was focused, and in it to win it. Submit wasn't the only hater on the team. There was also this pudgy Italian named Vinny, the ugliest looking guy I've ever seen—but the worst part about him, was his fucking obnoxious voice. He was also loud, and neither of them were great salespeople, I mean, Submit was probably the best one on the team before I came along, but things were changing. I met another guy on the team named Terell, who seemed very cool at first but more later about him. Then there was Tomas, who I liked the most. Tomas was a huge warrior-like Puerto Rican guy who was about 6 foot 5 and was by no means good at sales, which is probably why he's a cop now.

I would come in earlier than all of them and leave last. I was putting in 50 hours a week, I was ambitious, and I had the desire to win. At first, Tomas, Submit and I were all cool. We'd take Submit's Honda Civic, drive up to the gym and work out every day. Then they got me accustomed to buying Grilled Chicken Greek salads with extra feta. We were cool for a few months. I'm telling you I was on fire. I was the top salesperson on my team at one point. People didn't understand what the secret ingredient was that I had to offer; one thing I disliked was when Chris, the team manager would listen in on my phone calls to see how I was closing. I was really good and getting very arrogant as I was able to save lots of money. I remember one time someone made a wise remark, and I answered boldly "I'm captain of this ship!" But this didn't last. Of course, I was manic, and this mania could only last a few weeks or months tops. I rapid cycled, which gave me more unpredictable moods, but then all of a sudden I started getting depression, and I wasn't passionate about sales anymore. I didn't care; the work was repetitive, stupid, and they would hire monkeys if they could. Anyone could do the work.

The guys on the team were making fun of me and Submit and Vinny were the instigators of it. After the few months they worked alongside me they began to pick up on all my quirks, mannerisms, and oddities. They made fun of the fact that I pulled my eyelashes as a way to relieve stress and anxiety. I had what was known as Trichotillomania; this is an OCD disorder where the person repeatedly pulls hair and can't stop. It didn't matter if it was in front of others. Although it was embarrassing, I couldn't stop pulling—it made me feel better. They also made fun of my mannerisms and my personality.

They also made fun of the fact that I would set up phony meetings with non-execs, but low level people like janitors. They made fun of me for that. Let me just clarify this once and for all: When there's a lot of pressure on you to be the best at your craft, people tend to become desperate in these times, and desperate times call for desperate measures. The fact is, I'll be the first to admit it, I wanted to win so bad I was willing to do **anything** to win at all costs, and I jeopardized my reputation as a great salesperson not because I set phony meetings, but because those of my meetings that I set up in a last minute attempt to add to the scoreboard were rushed, and therefore, they weren't the quality of work that people normally expected from me. But those three idiots took it to another level and exaggerated the weakness of my performance.

I was working hard, putting in 50-60 hours a week just to reach my goal of 100 meetings in 90 days. Things got worse because I didn't like how loud and rowdy some of the guys on my team were. They were like high school jocks in the locker room. Didn't they know that this was a place of work? They hung up a basketball hoop on one of the cubicles and started dunking on it right as I was closing a deal. I almost closed, until the exec on the other line heard all the loud rowdiness and got upset. He said that my company didn't sound very professional, and he chose not to set up an introductory meeting with Ergonomics, my client. I was furious, and started yelling at Tomas, who was the loudest of them all having just made his dunk. I yelled at him to shut up and informed him that I just lost a sale because of him. I was so mad that I wanted to fight him, so I shouted to him to come outside and fight me. As I walked down the stairs, I began to slowly think. I didn't want to hit him, as I would lose my job if I did and I didn't really want to fight him, it was just my anger getting the best of me. Plus he was much bigger than me. He told me he wasn't going to hit me first, that I'd have to hit him but that I would regret it. All of my sales team were looking out the windows to see us fight, but it didn't happen. I told him that

I didn't want to fight him and explained that he just pissed me off and cost me a sale, but Tomas was my friend. We were workout buddies. People said that I chickened out of the fight afterward, but that was far from the truth. I hadn't needed to fight, I had just needed to express my feelings of intense anger and rage.

The fact was this company wasn't a professional workplace at all. Sure, they made money, but they hired people fresh out of college who weren't necessarily ready to work in a professional setting. I requested a change of seats because Submit, Vinny, and Tomas were terribly loud and they had begun affecting my sales performance in a negative way.

Anyway, I had one day left to hit the 100 meetings; anyone who has achieved great things knows that it puts a great pressure on them to win, to the point where you'll do anything to win. And so, I began setting up appointments with lower level execs, people who weren't qualified to talk to my clients. In the end, I was still two shy of meeting my 100 meetings quote. I didn't make it to become a Senior Inside Sales Rep, and it bruised my ego badly. From that day on, things changed.

I started the sales job March of 2007, and I lasted there eight months. After losing the opportunity to become a Senior Sales Rep, which I knew I had earned, my sales performance began to decline because I had started to get bouts of depression, really bad depressive moods that lasted for up to a few months. I began thinking how repetitive and boring the work was. I started to think that this wasn't the right job for me, and to continue calling countless times only to be rejected over and over again, this was getting to me. So I began talking to managers of other teams, as well as my sales friends like Jaime Blanch, who was a guy from the Philippines who was the only one loyal to me on my team. Well, word began spreading that

I wasn't happy there and I wanted other opportunities. I wanted to do a job where I didn't have to fight and struggle and be pressured every day to meet quotas which often weren't realistic. I started looking at other opportunities. I remember Laura, the marketing team manager, talked to me about possibly switching over to her team as a marketing specialist, but when I saw how boring the work they were doing was I politely declined.

Soon enough, November 2007 came, and Thanksgiving break was just around the corner. Everyone was excited to get a few days off for the Thanksgiving holiday. So the day before the break, around lunchtime, Chris called me over and says that they were letting me go due to my poor sales performance in the last few months. But they knew that I didn't want to be there any longer, so the way that I see it, they were doing me a favor by letting me go. At the time, I was pretty sad, as for the previous eight months sales had been my life. An older teammate saw me pack my things and knew that I was melancholy. He told me to go home, and drink a few cold beers, and that it'd make me feel better.

When I got back to Brookline, it wasn't fun to sit around and not do anything, but that's what I did, as I waited for Anette to get home from her job as a medical writer. I was jealous of her. She had a great, highly paid job, but most of all she had something that I lacked but wanted—a sense of purpose. I had nothing to do so I began lying in bed all day and drinking at a Chinese restaurant on Beacon St called the Golden Temple. In our studio in Brookline we were having problems with our neighbors because they partied a lot and we couldn't sleep. We decided to move back to Anette's Roslindale home where we lived in the basement for a few months. I got my first dog which I fostered. It was a one-year-old female brown Pitbull named Scarlett who I rescued. She came from an abusive home and was thrown out and abandoned on the streets to be homeless. She was a loyal dog to me-but she had aggression problems. When we would play fight, she attempted to bite at my neck and that's when I knew that there was a problem. She would never intentionally hurt me, but she also knew that I was her owner. I took care of her, I loved her, and so she stood by me and was my protector. I jogged the Jamaica Pond with Scarlett, I loved that dog, but things came to an end when one day I got home from work after working overnight and fell asleep. Well, Anette's brother lived on the second floor with his fiancé, Theresa, and one day Theresa came down to do the laundry. Next, I woke up in horror when I heard a loud shriek coming from the kitchen where the washer and dryer was. I jumped out of bed, and ran to see what was going on, only to find Theresa on the floor crying and shouting in pain at me because Scarlett had bitten her and taken off a chunk of her calf muscle. Theresa and I didn't particularly like each other, but what was worse was that she thought I had trained the dog to bite her. This was far from true. The truth is, that Scarlett was very protective of me and when Theresa came into our space she thought that she was an intruder, and attacked. What happened next absolutely crushed me. Chris (Anette's older brother) came down and when he saw what was happening, he yelled to me to call 911. I did, and the ambulance came and took Theresa to the hospital. Unfortunately, the cops were called, and they called Boston Animal Control, which said they would come to take Scarlett away to be euthanized. I wasn't okay with this and thought about leaving with Scarlett so that they couldn't take her. But in the end they did. So I lost the first dog I had ever owned and taken care of. I was saddened by this, but Anette got me a new puppy, a beagle. We named him Johnny 5. The dog was cute and charming, but it could never truly replace Scarlett.

Since my days at BSC, I began to develop an addiction, not only with alcohol but also with sleeping around. I did cheat on Anette, multiple times, even though she was so good to me allowing me to live rent free and caring for me. But I couldn't help myself. I blame my age, I was only 22 years old, and loved sex. First, I met up with a Chinese girl from English class at Bunker Hill. She was timid and met me at Forest Hills where she bought me fried rice from a Chinese restaurant. I picked her up, and we drove back to Anette's basement, where she took off her clothes and I fucked her. She was absolutely beautiful; when she took off her clothes she was in yellow lingerie, and she looked so good. This sex wasn't like the sex I was usually accustomed to—she was more petite, and so I was more delicate and passionate when we had sex. I got her off and when I finally entered her, she was super tight, and I loved every moment of it. We went from the mattress that me and my girlfriend slept on to the couch, where we fucked sitting up. After we were done, we ate our Chinese food and she left. Later on, Anette came home, and didn't suspect a thing.

Anette and I were happy to an extent. She would take me to her parents' house in Dennis, which was in the Cape. As a matter of fact, we'd go every weekend, and stay at this in-law apartment of a nice cottage that her parents owned in Dennis. What can I say about the Cape? It was peaceful and quiet... but too quiet for me. There was just nothing to do but hang around. I began going stir crazy and didn't like it. But there are some memories I had of spending time there with her that I truly will never forget. She took me to breakfast spots, like a members-only club called Sons of Erin that her father, was a member of. She took me to the beach, where I rollerbladed for a while and enjoyed the fresh air. But my favorite memory of the Cape, was when she took me to this chili contest at some bar. Rich, Anette's father, was an Army veteran, and he loved to drink Miller Lite. In fact, he had a problem. He just couldn't stop. He'd drink while he was doing work in the garage, or drink when he was gardening, it wouldn't just be at the bar. Anyway, I began to drink a lot again too, because I didn't see anything wrong with drinking beer. But the chili contest was really fun. We went around sampling different restaurants' chili; my favorite was the chili made with Guinness beer. This chili was something that I'd never had before; it was something special.

Christmas 2007 came and I had experienced the kind of Christmas that I had never experienced with my family. We woke up and opened our presents with the whole family on Christmas morning, and they were extremely generous. I got shirts, movies, all sorts of shit, and I didn't even get them anything! You see, I wasn't accustomed to getting presents or exchanging gifts or any of this stuff, and so it took me by surprise. My brother would later say that same thing about his family Christmases after he was married to his wife. He experienced a Christmas that we weren't used to. They showed us love and took joy in giving the gifts to us.

MAY 2008

I graduated Northeastern with my Bachelor's of Science Degree in Leadership in May of 2008, but the fact was that I was lost. Here I was, with a degree in a field that I knew nothing about and no idea what kind of a job I wanted to pursue. I began working at Walgreens as an Assistant Manager to keep busy. It was either the management position or a job at a preschool as a teacher's assistant. I lasted for three or four months. While I was there I had gotten into a car accident and my whole front bumper was off (don't worry, I was OK); as I was driving home through Mattapan and Blue Hill Ave in Dorchester to get back home to Roslindale, a state trooper pulled me over. He said that it was illegal to drive like this with the motor all open in the front. He asked what I did for work, and he almost towed me, so I lied to him, telling him that my cousin worked for the Boston Police. When he asked what they did there, I told him he was in internal affairs. I looked him dead in the eye when I answered him, and somehow, he believed every word I said. He got a bit afraid, and he let me go, telling me just to get that fixed.

In May I took Anette to the Barnes and Noble on Route 9 in Milton, and we went to the fiction section; as she was looking at the books on the shelves, I got down on one knee and proposed to her.

She teared up and said yes. She was so happy! I gave her a beautiful claddagh ring with an emerald stone inside.

The day that I graduated, Anette, my abuelita and parents were with me to celebrate. I had a party held in her parent's house and everyone from Zoya and the Russians to Dan Dicenso, Danny, my friend Dimitri, and all of Erika's friends came to celebrate. One thing you should know, is that Zoya was absolutely stunning. She reminded me of a Russian Cameron Diaz, and I had had a huge crush on her ever since we lived in Windsor Gardens. But I'll never forget the day that she told my brother that I was very good looking but too fat for her. Those words hurt me and have stuck with me to this day.

I began heavily drinking, because even though it was supposed to be a happy day, I felt like my father wasn't proud of me. I felt shamed, like my family being there wasn't in my best interest; they doubted me and I could feel it, especially from my father. I don't know if this makes sense but it felt like they were not authentically there for me. I began to drink, heavily, one beer after another. This girl Tanisha from Walgreens was there. She was really pretty, and at one point when the others were upstairs, I began to make out with here. She stopped kissing me and told me, "Oh it's like that huh?" I replied, "yeah." I drove her to some club in Hyde Park that she was going to, and she wanted me to come, but I told her I had to get back to the party. Anette and I were now engaged, and I felt guilty that I had continued to betray her by cheating on her behind her back. I felt especially guilty because I knew how good she had been to me. As we celebrated at the party, my brother posted on social media that I had graduated college, and he was so proud of me. I loved my brother to death. We were close, and I had looked out for him since we were kids. In fact we looked out for each other. It felt good to know that he was proud of me.

How did I do as an assistant manager at Walgreens? Well I didn't do badly in terms of managing my high school/college teammates. I was responsible for making sure the aisles were clean and all product was faced up and looked fresh. I did well at resolving customer disputes and providing high quality customer service, but I wasn't very good at counting up all the registers at the end of the night. It was hard to count up cash from four different cash registers. I'd be in the office in the process of counting money, when all of a sudden, I'd get a call for Mr. Paez to go to the photo dept for customer assistance. I kept messing up the balances and got written up for it. In the end, however, they didn't fire me because I kept fucking up the money, I got fired because I rushed and closed the store three minutes too early. Walgreens wasn't the job for me, but my problem was that I started noticing that I still couldn't hold a job for long, which made me really insecure and fearful that I was losing so many of the jobs that I worked at.

SEPT 2008

In September, 2008, Anette and I purchased our first house. It was a two-family in Stoneham. I gave her $10,000 to help with the down payment, but later found out that I wasn't on the deed. She set it up sneakily with her lawyer, and I didn't find out until the closing that I wasn't on the deed! I was upset; this was supposed to be my house too. It was a beautiful green Victorian on Gerry St in Stoneham, MA. We agreed that I'd live rent free. I even got my best friend Danny to live in the attic for only $400 a month to help Annette cover the mortgage. She found tenants for the first floor almost instantly. Everything seemed good, but it wasn't.

It was during this time that I got severely depressed. I wasn't working, I had no purpose. Anette was out at work the whole day and I was by myself. I spent most of my time sleeping because I didn't know what to do with myself. On weekends, Danny and I would party, along with Annette. I was drinking vodka heavily on weekends; one night I was so drunk that I fell down on the floor, face first into the dog's water bowl. It was embarrassing, and I needed help.

I had begun going to AA meetings and managed to be sober almost a year in 2006, but I had felt like the meetings weren't helpful enough; as much as I had the sense of connection with the people as well as a sense of community, it got hard to just not drink. So one day, I imbibed and before you know it I was drinking again.

We spent a lot of our time going out to eat as well as ordering pizzas from Andreas and roast beef sandwiches from Mike's Roast Beef. There was also Joe's American Bar and Grill, as well as an Indian restaurant, and during the week I'd go to the Chinese buffet on Main St. I often ordered more than one pizza when we ordered out. I binge ate, a recurring pattern for me my whole life it seemed.

Things weren't good between Anette and I. Due to some medical issues that she was having, she stopped having sex with me. She just didn't feel the desire anymore. This was not a good thing for me. I was a young guy, and I needed to have sex as much as I could. This was a big problem for me. So I began having sex with whatever woman I could pick up as often as possible. There was a girl that I met while she was working at a gas station, and I took her home one night when Anette was away at a work-related thing, and I drank beer with her, and then fucked her on our big queen-sized bed. She was a virgin, and she was a bit nervous but she said she wanted to lose her virginity to me. As I went inside her, I got more and more excited, and so I started going in fast and hard. It hurt her, but it felt so good for me to go fast. I never saw her again after that. Then there was Lydia, a beautiful petite Brazilian girl that I had met while working at Walgreens. She wanted me, and one day we had almost hooked up in the stock room, but nothing had happened. We kept in touch via social media, and one day Anette saw a flirty message from Lydia on my Myspace page. She wrote her back and scolded her for talking to someone who was engaged. They got into a little cat fight and that was the end of that. Another ex-partner messaged me and she saw the message. It said that I could do so much better, and Anette was clearly hurt by this. This was the beginning of our relationship's descent into hell.

Not only that, I began to resent her, and verbally abuse her to some extent. I'd call her a fat bitch when we argued, and I'd berate her, the same way that my father would berate me.

Anette urged me to go to the Mass General Hospital Bipolar Clinic to get diagnosed and admitted for Bipolar Disorder. So I set up a consultation with Dr. Deckersbach, a German doctor who asked me many questions about my moods and at the end gave me a diagnosis of Bipolar Disorder. I was relieved; things finally started to make sense; now we knew more about why I was the way I was. I could get help to help alleviate the intense rage, the wild mood swings, and the heavy drinking. Dr Deckerbach agreed to give me Cognitive Behavioral Therapy once a week, but I didn't like his style, and so I told him that. I did want someone to practice CBT on me and evaluate my distorted thinking patterns, all while being empathetic and really listening and acknowledging what I had said. Instead, he looked as if he didn't care; he had a cold, blank, stare and just asked how I could've thought about this differently. I didn't like him, so I told him so. And that was my mistake, my big mouth. When I told him that he was a terrible therapist, he actually kicked me out of the Bipolar Clinic, but at least I had a psychiatrist at the MGH Bipolar Clinic, Dr. Astrid Desrosier, who right away put me on several antipsychotics and mood stabilizers, including lithium, Klonopin and Xanax, help me with my panic attacks . I was mainly diagnosed with Bipolar Disorder, but I also had a big anxiety disorder, mainly social anxiety. It was great to work with Dr Desrosiers. She really listened to me and, based on what I told her my symptoms were and how I was feeling, she'd try me on new meds. I've been on everything imaginable. But now I was starting to have the tools to fight this terrible mental illness.

I once had an evaluation done at the Boston University Center for Anxiety and other Related Disorders. It was done by a team of psychologists, who asked me many questions about myself and my life; it lasted almost four hours! At the end, they gave me a long report about what I had: According to them, I had Bipolar Disorder, social anxiety disorder, generalized anxiety disorder, PTSD, and ADHD. Knowing these things helped because now I could work on them in therapy with Marty. I continued going to West Roxbury to see Marty, but eventually he told me that my wounds were unfortunately too deep for him to heal, and that I needed a more intense form of therapy. So he terminated our therapeutic relationship. I was bummed out. Marty had been my favorite therapist, and I had been seeing him since 2005-2009. He helped me a lot with my anger issues and anxiety. We did however, discuss potential careers for me and concluded that I should go take my prereqs for nursing at Bunker Hill Community College so I enrolled back at Bunker Hill for the start of the 2009 Spring semester in January.

I enrolled in Anatomy I and II, took all these courses plus Microbiology and Statistics, as well as Drug Calculations. I aced every class except the stupid Drug Calculations. The formulas were simple and there were a lot of conversions that you had to do but I had difficulty with this course.

Things were not going well for Anette and me. The breaking point was when I told her to meet me at the Hong Kong Café in Harvard Square in Cambridge. I was taking Red Cross classes to become a certified nursing assistant and met up with her after the class. I was the first one to get there, so I ordered a drink. And then another drink, and a third. By the time Anette arrived she was almost an hour and a half late! Just as she was coming towards me smiling with her arms open to see me I flipped out on her instead, yelling at her in front of the whole bar. I made her cry, and she was really embarrassed. I was angry with her at the time, but later, when I calmed down, I realized that what I had done was embarrassing. Hell, I was embarrassed at my actions. But then I asked her where she had been, and told me she had been with her friend, a male friend. She said nothing happened between them but later I found out she had made out with him! These were trying times and I was a man of faith but times were hard. She wasn't the only one though.

I went out with some friends from Bunker Hill. It was Brian and Celyne, a French older woman. I met her at the bookstore at Bunker Hill; she worked there. I was interested in her. She was smart, beautiful and charming, and I wanted her. But I was with Anette. We partied at some bars downtown, then we went walking through Boston Common to get back to our car, where the conversation transferred to sex talk. Celyne was drunk (we all were) and she started singing, "pussy, pussy, pussy!" We were all joking, having fun, I dropped Brian off then drove Celyne home to her apartment. When we got in, we just went at it, making out intensely-. We didn't even make it to her bedroom; we tore each others' clothes off and I fucked her hard from behind. She wanted me to wear a condom but I didn't. I went bare. She was surprisingly tight for a 36year old woman. In the heat of the passion we were both drunk off our asses and fucking on the living room floor. It was so hot.

2009

2009 was the worst year of my life. I say this because I had no direction, didn't know what I wanted to do, and I'd say this further killed my self esteem and made me feel extremely hopeless about my future. I couldn't hold a job. I had 14 jobs that year! I worked at an assisted living facility, but the director was a dick and changed my status to part-time from full-time because I had written that a client "shat all over himself." I should have been more professional, but I was young and I didn't know any better. I would bike from Stoneham to Lynnfield, which was about a half hour on bike. But I left that job too. For the remainder of 2009 I would work 14 shit jobs like security, where I was treated like shit by managers and other higher ups. I remember I was at this one company where I worked in Billerica, at Lantheus Medical Imaging. They could only give me overnight weekend shifts but I accepted them, and it wasn't bad working there. Every two hours I had to do a tour; I had this little electric golf caddy that I'd drive around in at 3am in the morning! I did donuts in the snow when it snowed and had a lot of fun, that thing actually had some power! But my job was to do a secure tour of all the buildings and there were six of them. One building in particular, was a training center where firefighters trained. It was spooky because there were dummies on the ground and it looked like a factory. I always ran when I did that building. But the part of the tour that scared me the most was this power strip that was out in the middle of the dark woods. There were coyotes in these woods, and I quickly did what I was supposed to do and left on my little electric powered go cart.

None of these jobs worked. My friend Rommel, who was taking science courses with me at the community college, hooked me up with a job with Securitas. I worked under this pretty cool Lebanese guy named Bob; he got me a job at a Days Inn Hotel. I loved working there, and best of all I had three 12-hour shifts on weekends, so I got the rest of the days off. I loved it there because I had a lot of freedom but the only rule was, I couldn't go inside the rooms of any clients. There was this white woman at the front desk who always wanted to have a reason to catch me doing something bad. She was a miserable woman. Anyway, I met a couple of gorgeous women there, but I'll never forget one Puerto Rican and Dominican woman named Ida. Ida had like four little kids running around and she always talked to me and got flirty. One day, I told her something sexual, like "You look good I want you," when she replied, "oh honey you can have me anytime you want to." My dick grew six times larger in that moment, and we went into her room; she undid my belt and whipped out my dick. I was in full security uniform so she was extremely turned on. I ripped of her clothes and fucked her with my security badge on and everything, the only thing down was my pants. She had an onion booty that must have made grown men cry! It was the ninth wonder of the world; goddamn it was great! I fucked her rough and hard doggystyle—it was the best. She had a fat ass that bounced up and down and was moaning. I told her to call me "papi" during sex, and she did. I came. It was such a great orgasm. I was sweating and I was at peace with the world, myself and all around me. Me and Ida began meeting every weekend both Fridays and Saturday when I was do my "rounds and security checks." The sex was so good, and whenever I worked she be sure to cook me a plate of arroz con pollo with beans. Latinas are great people, not only as lovers but as partners. They are loyal, extremely caring and nurturing, and they care for the other person's needs. I definitely appreciated Ida.

Anyway, I ended up getting fired from the security job; remember the white lady at the front desk that I told you about? Well, she reviewed the hotel CCTV and saw me going into rooms multiple times during my shift. There was another older gentleman who worked there who knew what I was doing but he looked away. It wasn't him that got me fired, but the lady. I had my friend who lived there slash her tires. He told me that she was crying and scared; she knew that it was done through me, but there were no cameras there so she had no proof. I was upset, but my boss just transferred me to another site, part-time at the ICA-the Institution of Contemporary Art, where young white privileged women who worked there would talk down to me simply for standing there guarding the paintings and shit. They wanted me to do something other than just stand there. The banquet staff would let us security officers into the kitchen to dig in on the leftovers. They treated us worse than everyone else and I realized that I wasn't in the right field of work. Eventually I got fired from the Securitas job because I didn't come in for my shift one day, but it wasn't entirely my fault. I had an unorganized manager who scheduled me different places on different days and then this led to me being confused, and I thought I wasn't working that day. I was losing faith in myself when it came to keeping a job and felt like my life was going nowhere.

My father finally lost his temper one day when he had to buy me glasses at Costco because I didn't have any money. Anette was with us, and he yelled at her, "He had $30,000 saved last year; where did it all go?" He was implying that she had been taking money from me. Anette didn't play around. She left Costco and later told me that she didn't ever want that man in my house again. My father did care, but his problem was that he was impulsive, and couldn't control his emotions. When he had something to say, he said it.

Also, I didn't have a car at this point, so Anette helped me by loaning me some money to purchase a lease—I got the 2009 Nissan Altima 2.5S. For the time that I had the car it was nice, but eventually I lost all sources of income and had no way to make the monthly payments, so I went with my father to a dealership in Medford to sell it at a loss of $2000. I was seriously about to cry when I looked my father in the eye and asked him to please help me. He did; he paid the two grand, but he never forgot about it. He was the type of person to criticize me for all my faults and mistakes. He didn't understand that failure and making mistakes was a part of life; that is how we grow, I didn't understand at that time either and felt that I was a total failure and wasn't meant to hold down a job.

Later in the year, Anette convinced me to take classes over at Red Cross to become a Certified Nursing Assistant and gain experience. I met a lot of cool young people from many different parts of the world, but this is where I met my future wife, Ann. Ann was 11 years older than me, and I thought she was beautiful. She was an immigrant from Trinidad who had no green card. I remember we hung out one night; it was me, Danny and Ann. We met her at the Ashmont station and walked to her house from there. We started drinking and Danny left. We just talked about life. She had a small one-bedroom on Argyle Terrace in Dorchester, where she had the bedroom, and her cute son (who was nine years old when I met him) slept on the futon in the small living room. We began drinking wine one night when her son wasn't home and that led to sex. I began cheating on Anette with Ann for a little while, but it wasn't until June 2009, when Michael Jackson died, that Anette had officially broken up with me. I could still live there, but now I was sleeping in the attic.

Danny wasn't right. He wasn't okay. He was isolating, he liked being by himself, and he talked to himself. I knew that he needed mental health help, but he didn't have insurance. I worked on getting him on Mass Health. One night, when I was sleeping up there, he brought over some gay friend, who kept checking me out and wouldn't let me sleep. I instantly kicked him out. But then Danny kept playing with me and wouldn't let me sleep. It was extremely odd what happened. He was in the room next door, and I was sleeping on the floor, when every five or ten minutes Danny would come over tickling me and waking me up and giggling like a little school girl. I told him many times to stop, only he didn't. This lasted for a good 20 minutes, and I got really upset, so I got my belt and I started whipping him, the same way that my dad had whipped me. He got the message and went to bed. But I had hurt my best friend, and felt really bad, even though he was acting like he had an episode or something. He was delusional and it took me a while to see it but I finally did. When I did see it, I knew that he needed serious help.

I couldn't sleep up there in the attic anymore. Not only was it extremely hot, but I was afraid of what Danny would do. He was acting extremely weird. So Anette let me sleep in her bed. She was the one that officially broke up with me. But I was being hopeful, I thought I could work hard and turn things around, but it simply did not happen that way. Worst part of it all was that she wrote up a lawyer like document which served as a contract with all the money that she had to pay back minus what I owed her. What's worse she made me sign it. It really made me see her true colors. There was no loyalty nor love for me anymore, and so I signed it. I gave her $10k that I saved from working hard which she used toward the down payment. I finally figured out that I wasn't even listed on the deed which was total bullshit. She basically used the money as an interest free loan! I gave her Danny, and he was paying her $400 a month, but it still wasn't enough for her. Then what made things worse, a TV that I bought she began crying for me to please leave it for her as well as Johnny5 (our Beagle). That was rightfully my dog, but because she manipulated me by crying (something women have been doing to me since the beginning of time, first by my mother) so I gave in.

In September of 2009, I moved back home. I remember the day very clearly. As I went back to my parents house on Sanborn Ave in West Roxbury, my dad sat down next to me and I just began crying uncontrollably. I truly loved Anette and was in complete disbelief and shock that this had happened to me. I was sitting there crying, and at least my father "attempted" to console me. But he showed empathy for one of the first times in my life. He told me, "Jasio, she wasn't the right girl for you," and just sat there with me, and by him just being there it made all the difference in the world to me. I appreciated that he did that. It was one of the few times when he let his guard down.

You already know what happened to me after that in September, don't you remember? When I smashed the beer bottle into the window at Grand Canal Pub and broke the window and cut open my hand and almost got arrested but didn't because the owner didn't want to press charges cuz I cried like a little girl and apologized? Well, this was a crucial point in my life. I was lost, and I didn't know what to do about it, or where to go, or even where to begin. To be honest, my mental health was declining for a long time I just never did anything about it. And here I was, 25 years old and didn't have a clue what I wanted to do for a living. All I know what that 2009 was a terrible year for me-I had lost the love of my life, was just rebounding with Ann to avoid living at home and because of my fears of being alone. I was extremely vulnerable during this time. But the worst part of it all, I had worked over 14 jobs that I was unsuccessful at and many of them I left or got fired. They were mainly a lot of security jobs, I sold Kirby vacuums, worked at grocery stores-after the sales job, honestly, I did whatever job I could find.

In September of 2009, I had moved in with Ann to her small apartment in Ashmont, a part of Dorchester that at the time was only beginning to become gentrified. I had been sleeping with her all summer, and I really liked her at first. I continued my pattern of moving in with women that I didn't know very long only to escape living with mainly my father.

My mother helped me get back on track. My mother worked in Human Resources for Harvard University, and got me a job as a Staff Assistant at the Harvard School of Dental Medicine. My resume says staff assistant but I was really just a phone operator. So my mother set me up with an interview with Monique, the Director of HR for the dental school, along with Catherine Lane, the Director of Clinical Operations at the dental school. I knew that I was representing my mother, and so I wanted to make her proud. She went through a lot for me to get me this interview. I charmed both of them, and when they asked if I spoke Spanish I said that I speak it but not fluently. I was being honest, I did speak Spanish-un pocito.

JANUARY 2010

My first day was January 3. I arrived at the Harvard School of Dental Medicine, where I went into the building, checked in, and was greeted by Catherine, who took me down to the phone operators area and I first met Tisha, who was one of the phone operators. Next, Clara came in. She was a privileged young white girl who thought she ran the dental school. She was prissy and not a very nice person, especially to me. Clara was someone who I absolutely dreaded working with for my time at the dental school. She thought of herself as the "boss" when she was the same paygrade as me. I found out that the reason she acted all entitled was because her sister worked in HR. Both of the women that I worked with there didn't teach me anything, were easily annoyed with me, and displayed passive aggressive behaviors when I did things wrong. Right off the bat, they didn't give me a fair chance, and things turned ugly when Clara found out that I didn't speak fluent Spanish. She told Dr Gallucci, one of the prosthodontists that I lied at my interview about speaking Spanish just to get the job. Worst part of this is, she had the audacity to say this right in front of me! I was super enraged and embarrassed. Tisha could be cool, but was extremely moody and had a bad attitude. She would come into the office angry, like she didn't want to be there. Both of them sided against me, and they wouldn't even train me! So half the time I didn't know what the hell I was doing. It was like that for the first month. But I stayed strong. I knew that I may not have knew all the doctors and where to schedule patients yet, and for which practice, but I knew my strength-it was providing a high quality of customer service to the patients, and this didn't go unnoticed.

After about a month, things were not going good because of Clara and Tisha. We were not only not getting along, but when I asked questions they got mad. Pam, the assistant manager, would come in and say that there was so much tension in our section that you could cut it with a knife!

I told Catherine Lane, and we set up a team meeting. At the meeting, nobody knew why the fuck we were there except me. Catherine asked me to start it off, and so I said. "I arranged for this meeting today because I wanted to diffuse whatever tension was among us and I wanted us to all get along." Of course, Miss Entitled Clara immediately got upset and felt that I had betrayed them. Fuck that bitch, I absolutely hated her, but she said, "We don't need to be here and you going behind our back like this is blah blah blah and we will never hang out outside of work." Now when she said that, do you think that I gave two fucks that she didn't want to hang out with me outside of work?! I'm surprised this girl had anyone to hang out with period. She was a stuck up bitch who needed to get checked. Me and her went back and forth, and at one point in the meeting, she was like "Can I finish?" I replied angrily, "Go ahead!" At least now Catherine and Pam the other manager could see what I was dealing with. Tisha kept quiet throughout the entirety of the meeting. Then, Clara started saying that they tell me things over and over again and I don't remember and keep asking them to help Next thing you know, Catherine began talking about the Law of 7.

"Does anyone know what the law of 7 is?" She said. "A person needs to be told information up to 7 times before their brain retains that information." The ultimate result was that we all agreed to work as a team. The more that I was practicing the better I got at the job but working with the both of them was a pain in the ass. They would give me anxiety, and I couldn't focus at times because they were talking. They also used passive aggressive behaviors to make me feel intimidated.

Things got better after my mother made an appearance to tea time at the Harvard School of Dental Medicine. It seemed that once people found out that Margaret was my mother, everyone was much nicer to me, including the two women that I worked with.

I spent a lot of time going out to lunch with my mother, she was my best friend. We'd go up to the park overlooking the city in Mission Hill and eat lunch there. I spent most of my lunches venting to her about my problems at work, and how stressed I was because of those two. My mother's mother was a schizophrenic and her father was an alcoholic whom they left when she was a little girl. My mother had similar anxiety to me, as well as chronic worrying, or Generalized Anxiety Disorder (GAD) as the experts referred to it. She used to nag me so much, she actually made things worse because she wouldn't stop no matter how much I pleaded with her to. She could also be moody as well, and say things that would intentionally hurt my feelings. I'm not proud to admit this, but I've actually put hands on her because I couldn't take her nagging to me. I've pinched her to stop her from casting her anxieties on me or said nasty things to make her cry (because I knew that that would stop her from continually nagging me).

In March of 2010, I moved Ann and her son to a 2-bedroom apartment just over in the next building. At first the little kid was adorable. He'd play with me and he'd show me how bright he was, but that all changed and as time went on he grew stubborn and lazy, a trait that I did not like to see in anybody. His mother began asking him to ask me to buy him things, which he did ALL the time. To me, I thought of him as a spoiled little shit who got his way anytime he wanted. Anyway, I remember when we were moving she flipped out on me, and it was like a deranged insane in the membrane flip out. She started yelling at me because of a simple request that I had told her. She was tired and wanted to be left alone, especially when she was stressed. She yelled for me to leave the house, and I did. That right there was a big warning flag that I should not have been with her, but I was afraid of being alone, and that's the truth. In May of 2010, only 2 months of living with her, I announced that I was moving out to live on my own. The truth was, Ann had a temper and lots of emotional baggage, which was evident by her outbursts (scary outbursts I might add) that had scared. Perhaps we rushed into things. That last night together, we both cried. But she understood that I had to go and experience living on my own.

I rented a room at a Polish man's house on Hinckley St in Dorchester. It was good for a while, I brought women home sometimes and the guy got mad when he heard the noise from us fucking. During these 3 months that I lived here, I really lost a significant amount of weight. I ran everyday, and ate healthy choice chicken noodle soups for dinner. The Polish lady that lived there was worried about me, and told me to go to Euromart, a Polish store, and pickup some gowombki (stuffed cabbage filled with ground meat covered with a tomato sauce on top). I did try that, and they were delicious, but I stayed true to my diet of chicken noodle soup.

Meanwhile, the guy, Piotrek was his name, was extremely cheap and anal. When I bought a toaster to toast stuff he unplugged it and wrote me a note that this consumes too much electricity! This guy was insane. Eventually he told me to move out, and so my parents and brother all helped me move. I was angry with the landlord and began yelling at him. I almost punched him in the face but my mother got int the middle of us and I couldn't do anything. So I packed up my things and moved to another house renting a room from some Columbians. But the room was tiny, the mattress that I bought from BJ's barely fit in there, and so I called Ann to help me move the mattress and put it on top of the car. I began thinking, that there was nobody else that I could call to help me in any situations-my parents didn't want to help, I felt isolated and completely alone. But when I called Ann she was the only person that came... and I really appreciated that. It seemed that she was the only one that I could count on.

I really loved Ann because at the beginning she was good to me and at the same time I knew that she was struggling, trying to make it in the U.S. without a green card. So, the issue was that she was working under the table for a Jewish client in Brookline, and when he died, she was left out of work. She was extremely worried, about her future here, raising her son, and about where she'd find her next job. Of course, I felt like my purpose in life was to help others. "When I give I give myself," said poet Walt Whitman. This was my mentality. I was depressed and going through a lot of things in my life but I wanted to help her and her son. I knew that if I married her, we could go to an immigration lawyer and finalize the green card in about 4 to 6 months, and she would be able to get a job legally, on the books. And so on September 2010, I asked her to marry me. It was so corny. We were in Dorchester Heights in the park near Marion Manor where I used to work as a CNA, in Southie. Anyway, she must not have liked the ring because she didn't even seem thrilled, but she said yes. We set the wedding to November 2010 in two months and went to Father Finney at the church in Dorchester so that he could orchestrate it for us. We wanted to get married at the church. That night, we went to get my father's blessing. He spoke to Ann and he tried telling her that I was mentally ill, and that now wasn't the right time, that I needed to get better. She then replied that she loved me and understood that my mental health was suffering. Things got ugly when she got upset at my father because he insisted that she not marry me and raised her voice to him. He didn't like that, and my brother really didn't like that, because he came in screaming at her. My father kicked her out, and I followed.

Then came November, the day before the wedding, my father and I went up to Millenium Park in West Roxbury. We took a long walk and my father tried to talk me out of marrying Ann. He tried to explain that she was just using me for a green card, that she didn't love me. I'll never forget what he told me he said, "Where are your balls?" It seemed like my whole family was telling me not to marry her because they saw it for what it was-she was just using me. But at the time I didn't see it that way, and I told him that I loved her and I wanted to help her.

That night, I had major anxiety. I met up with a friend from high school and went out to a club in Boston and danced and drank a bit. She wanted to fuck. So I was like, why not...I figured it was my last night as a bachelor before I got married and so we drove around Boston and both of us were horny but we had nowhere to go, and so I pulled over at the Moakley Park Track in South Boston, right off of the rotary there. We made it to the track and in the middle of the fucking field we took off our clothes and started fucking-at 2am in the morning! Problem is, that it was November and if you're from

Boston you know how cold it is during these winter months! My erection faded and I didn't last long at all! My partner was disappointed but hey, it's that Boston weather! What else can I say?

On the day of the wedding the next day I was extremely hesitant and apprehensive about marrying her. I tried to talk to Ann but she wasn't having it. I asked her if it was okay if I followed my father's wishes and not get married that day, and postpone it to a later date, she wasn't okay with that. She pretty much demanded that I marry her now and wasn't willing to compromise at all. So I pretty much caved in. Her fucking Uncle Albert kept calling to reassure me that I'm marrying into a great family, that his niece was a good woman but deep down I knew something wasn't right. I picked up my best man Dan Dicenso, who was one of my good friends from back in the days at Bridgewater State College, but to be honest, during this point of my life, I had no friends...as a matter of fact, since I left Bridgewater and after I finished my studies at Northeastern University, I was pretty much a loner. I spent as much time as I could occupying myself with work but I only used that as an outlet to mask the real problem that I've had most of my life, that chronic loneliness. I guess what I'm trying to say is that I picked Dan out of necessity and desperation, because my best friend, my brother-followed my father's orders and didn't go to the wedding, and so he declined to be my best man. Anyway, I was grateful that I had Dan in my corner he put me at ease a little bit. When we arrived at St. Mark's Parish in Dorchester, I felt ashamed. All of her family was there with their fake smiles and not ONE person showed up from my family or even gave me their blessing! This would continue to hurt me for years, and I'd struggle with this. So we got married, we went back to the apartment that we had on Argyle Terrace near Ashmont, and she had cooked some bullshit for everyone to enjoy. I remember that it pained me so much, that while her manipulative uncles which I despised were in the living room enjoying themselves and laughing and talking loudly with each other, I was alone in my tux in my bedroom, just sitting on the bed and thinking about what a terrible mistake I did. I didn't love her, I was in love with the idea of being in love, but for years after I pretended that everything was okay, but in time, you would see that this wasn't a good marriage, at all. I held a lot of anger in especially because of my parents who made it a point to not show up to the wedding. I was very hurt and resentful because of this. I tried to get at least my mother to come but she sided with my father, and that hurt even more. My brother was also under my father's spell. I also found out that my parents actually went to the priest to try to stop the wedding from happening, but he did not listen to their complaints. For as long as I could remember, my parents were control freaks, and when they didn't get what they wanted it drove them crazy, especially my father, who had the ability to win over people easily with his charisma.

In the new year, a Cape Verdean co-worker from the Dental School wanted to rent out her basement apartment to me for $950 a month. I moved most of my stuff in, but eventually decided that this wasn't the right decision. I began thinking, why rent when I can own my own house?

I started talking to Ann and suggested that instead of paying rent we should buy a house. I worked 56 hours a week to get approved for a mortgage, working incredibly hard fulltime during the week at Harvard and as a concierge/doorman on weekends. I would do this until I saved enough money to purchase our first home, on Wayland St right in Roxbury, MA, in April 2011. This was my first home, and I was very excited. I saved up almost $8000, while Ann only gave me $3000 to put down towards the down payment of my first house.

I put it in my name only, my lawyer made sure of it. But I guess that when you're married "what's yours is mine and vice versa" and I absolutely hated this. I felt that it was MY home that I worked hard for, and Terellp down it wasn't love, it was more so a business partnership that I used to my advantage to help me pay MY mortgage. I used her to my advantage and she used me to her advantage, it was a mutual business partnership, nothing else. The I love you's, the fake tears, all that was fake, and meant nothing as I would later find out.

When we first moved in, even on the first day, we were both very afraid of the environment. We thought about selling the house back as we had a week to do that, but in reality I wasn't going to let that happen. I was told that this was "gang territory" and that I should stay inside and lock all doors and windows when the sun set and nightfall came. The house was small but it was big enough. It had 2 rooms upstairs, and a basement. But you could tell this wasn't a good neighborhood. There were bullet holes in my vinyl siding, sneakers hanging up from the street lamp, and lots of noise-I hate noise. The very first things I noticed on the day that we moved in was these teenagers that were curious about who we were, and they leaned on my car and watched us move. I knew this was my first lesson in being respected, and so I assertively asked the kid to please get off my car. He complied and was cool about it. So I ended up getting a Siberian husky and this made me an instant hit. I moved into the hood when everyone else fought to move out. But the house was only $156k and was very close to my job at Harvard, so along with my mother's advice, I bought it. Anyway, back to my story. My dog, a female Siberian Husky puppy named Simba got a lot of attention. Gangs in cars would pull over and ask where they could buy a wolf like that! Or they'd say, "Yo there go the nigga with the wolf dog!" This was actually how I first got introduced to the leader of the Bloods gang Carlos, and his gang. They all came to know me very well and liked me enough to know that I was a standup guy who was chill and non-judgmental. I later found out that the house next door where Carlos lived was the gang's headquarters. They would beef there, there'd be parties with bitches and guns, and lots of Henny and marijuana smoke, and commotion going on there. Carlos was in his early 20s when I first met him and I thought he was a good kid in a bad environment. He was charismatic, down to earth and very humble, and loved that I liked his Cape Verdean family so much. His father was the biggest alcoholic on the block, and when he drank he'd disturb our whole street by yelling in the middle of the night, or stumbling on other peoples' porches and damaging property, but for as long as I knew him, he was a good and peaceful man. His mother was very kind as well, offering us rides when we didn't have a car to Stop and Shop, in Grove Hall.

One night, I met took Ann to a club in Worcester where I met up with an acquaintance, we'll call him Don. He was also the President of Men Integrated in Brotherhood back in college at BSC, and he seemed cool, but later I found out this guy was a total loser who did not like me very much, why? I never knew...which was strange because both him and I were a lot alike. Anyway, I went out to the club and danced had fun, but drank a lot as usual, and this wasn't good, because I had to drive back to Roxbury at 2am. So, I'm very drunk, and usually I was an excellent drunk driver but not tonight, because I had been speeding to get onto the highway and I crashed my car into the guard rail and it did not look good at all! The whole driver side fender was damaged, with a large chunk of it hanging off. It looked terrible! But I was determined to get home. I knew that If a Statie had pulled us over that night, I would've easily gone to jail. This is why I didn't bother calling AAA for a tow. I just drove straight back to Boston with my tiny Corolla severely damaged. I was extremely lucky, because had the police pulled us over, I would have probably not only gotten arrested for a DUI, but gone to jail. I took many chances playing chicken with death, and so far I had won, but how long would this last for? When we got home I didn't have money to repair it and so I drove it around like that for a while. This is how I learned that Carlos's father, was an excellent mechanic, and he could fix up that car for me. So I paid him to fix up the car, but later found out that instead of spending the money on parts and paint supplies for the vehicle, he spent most of my money on booze. And I grew more annoyed with him day after day, and let him know that I needed that car fixed asap. He was holding it week after week and I needed the car for work and other things. Then he'd demand more money, and I gave him a little bit more. When he finally fixed the car, It had been about 3 weeks that he had worked on it before I finally got it back and I spent too much money, it would've been easier to just get it taken care of by insurance. Anyway, Carlos and I became friends instantly. I liked him and he liked me because I hired his father to help me fix up my car. For the first 3 years was terrifying living there-Boston Police District B2 was there outside Carlos's house surrounding it constantly. I even saw the SWAT Team there. Often times they'd block the whole street. TALK ABOUT RUDENESS OF POLICE and how they accused me of stealing a laptop and I invited them in the house. There's a lot that the hood and in general poor people need to learn about the criminal justice law. For example, the police CANNOT by any means enter your home without a warrant, unless you invite them in (in which case I did). They woke up my stepson at like 1am and he had to explain that he didn't have any laptop, and so they left...but they didn't believe us. Then, one of them kept ringing my doorbell even though I answered and was angry about it. He did it for absolutely no reason whatsoever.

The SWAT Team would come multiple times with their big ass guns and block the whole street. This would happen when Carlos's ankle bracelet would go off. He was a felon, at around 23 years old, and has been to prison. Anyway, one night I was trying to leave and this cruiser was parked in front of my parking garage. I asked the SWAT officer if he could move his car and he gave me an attitude.

Another time someone was murdered right in front of my house, while my wife at the time and stepson were watching frozen. That's another problem, is lack of male father figures and all the violence that these kids witness. The guy that murdered the other man was arrested, and I was told that he was my neighbor, who drove a purple Chrysler. It's funny, I would give him daps all the time, never knew that I was shaking hands with a murderer.

I know the gangs were doing some bullshit, but I was cool with everybody, and never asked what was going on. Carlos would invite me up to his room to smoke, I'd bring Heineken beers and share them with others. Then, Carlos showed me a gun-a 9 millimeter Smith and Wesson with the serial scratched off. I held it in my hand and he asked for it back right away and was worried that I'd accidentally shoot it. That's another problem in inner cities. You ask, how are these 14- and 15-year-olds getting access to these guns? Well, the answer is New Hampshire, and other places where you don't need background checks.

There was an instance when I saw a young teen who was unstable-I saw him from my window walking down the street holding and pointing the handgun at oncoming traffic! I was in shock and disbelief and called the police immediately.

Things were very dangerous in our neighborhood, and I worried, and I also felt very bad that my stepson had to witness all this shit. We had to lock the doors when night time came because that's when bad things happened in the street. You could get robbed, or worse, even killed, for looking at somebody the wrong way.

One Saturday night in the summer, Carlos was beefing with some other gang member and the guy was yelling loud. You could tell that he was in a rage. And the thing that bothered me is-he didn't respect that there were neighbors and families with kids that were trying to sleep. He acted as if they didn't exist and continued being a disturbance. It got worse, he was drunk, and ended up climbing on my back porch because it connected through to Carlos's house. So he climbed up my porch up to where my bedroom window was and began shouting from there at Carlos's brother. And that's when I had enough, and I called 911. This is bullshit, I realized that the reason that nobody cares about the community is because I found out that 70% rent, and only 30% of the people in that neighborhood owned homes, and so the others didn't care about the community. They littered near my house bigtime, throwing bottles and Doritos wrappers and even used car parts on my property line, near my fence. Criminal justice books described it as "Broken Windows Theory" that we learned at school about-that if a community is impoverished with poverty and you don't fix up the neighborhood, people will continue to trash it. There was no respect for our "community." Many people didn't like me, it was reverse racism. But I felt it. A lot of people felt that I didn't belong there. Story of my life!

Back to the guy that climbed up my back porch. The police had arrived but of course the guy and everyone else had scattered, and so they didn't find anything and left. A few minutes after the police left, the guy started yelling outside my window because he knew that I was the one that called the police on him. I did not dare to reply back to him, as I was inside the house and if I confronted him I probably would've gotten shot at. He stood outside my window for a good 10 minutes just yelling profanities and threatened to kill me. By this point I was extremely paranoid. I constantly stared out the window to see if anybody was outside the house, or when I parked the car before I got out I because I thought something or wanted to see why ambulance or police were on my block. Even when I arrived home at night, before I'd get out of my car I'd look around to make sure nobody was hiding under my porch or around my back parking lot. It even got to the point that I was online looking to buy a bulletproof vest because I was scared that someone would shoot at me.

Eventually I had enough. I decided that I'd be screwed since I did not have protection and most of the people in my neighborhood did. Why should they carry guns illegally when I was a U.S. citizen and could. Matter of fact, I could obtain one legally. It was my right as the 2nd Amendment states. So I went to the Boston Police Department Headquarters on 1 Schroeder Plaza in Roxbury and applied for a gun permit. I was called in, the detective there did a background check on me, took my picture as well as my fingerprints, and sent me on my way. The whole NCIS Background check is bullshit, because I suffered from Bipolar and was mentally ill, and I still got my gun permit approved! The way it works is, you fill out a form where it asks you questions. Well one of the questions was, "Have you ever been INVOLUNTARILY committed to an inpatient psychiatric ward?" I answered no, since it was the truth. But I had voluntarily checked into a hospital before, but they didn't ask that? You see-it's pretty easy for someone who is unstable to obtain his permit, and go buy 10 different guns. Gun selling is a business, and we live in a capitalistic society and so people want to sell guns. Gun dealers are happy to sell me a gun, and so I feel a big thing that needs to happen is they need to have stricter background checks on people so that the guns do not end up getting into the hands of the wrong people. Even if you look for guns online, you'd discover its extremely easy to get one.

As soon as I got my permit and paperwork in the mail, I went to a gun shop in Woburn, and bought my first gun. It was a Smith and Wesson M&P Shield 9MM handgun. It was small, so it could be easily concealed. When the guy asked me if I wanted target practice fake bullets or the real ones, I told him real-I remember he gave me a scared look but I meant business. If I felt threatened I'd let it go off. I didn't give a fuck! I carried that gun everywhere, even once had it in my car at the Salem State parking lot which was a big no no. But more on Salem State Grad School later! I even showed the gun to my friend D and his fiancé.. I asked him how to load the bullets into the clip because I couldn't figure out how to squeeze those suckers in there. He acted like he was a pro at it but was able to show me.

Marriage goes South

I don't know if Ann ever loved me, but she did try to accompany in the beginning but she was also unstable. When we first moved in, we were in bed and she was extremely disrespectful, calling me names and shouting at me, and so I slapped her. I'll be honest, I'd NEVER hit a woman before and never will again, but she wasn't a good woman. She was stubborn and hard headed. Anyway, I slapped her, I'll admit it. She screamed at the top of her fucking lungs and tried to grab and squeeze my balls. After about half an hour of her going absolutely crazy, I told her that I wanted a divorce. She began to cry, saying "Please don't leave me Jan." I had enough of her. She had mood issues too, plus she was 11 years my senior and so she could've been going thru menopause and could be extremely emotional. So I made amends with her and she apologize as did I, and we moved on. I was so foolish, thinking that everything was okay.

In the beginning in 2011 when I first moved in with her, things were always a little shaky but she tried. What I didn't like about her was the fact that on holidays, especially Thanksgiving and Christmas, she'd make Rum Punch and get drunk and cook. She cooked huge dishes of turkey and Caribbean foods such as okra and chicken feet which I couldn't understand how someone could eat that bullshit-there was no meat on it! That was her thing, cooking, and cooking a lot. I didn't like it because there'd be smells and then lots and lots of food and therefore lots and lots of dishes to clean. The worst part of it was, she neglected me. She'd leave me in the bedroom alone and leave both me and her son to watch TV for hours. The son already had emotional problems because he felt abandoned since she worked all the time. She blamed me because apparently, I had been taking all of her time which wasn't true. The truth was that we were a married couple, and was it so bad that I wanted her to invest time in me? I liked long walks at night and at first she accompanied me but then was too tired. Anyway, I did feel abandoned by her a majority of the time and this was a big red flag. The other red flag was her bad temper. She would yell at you and be completely disrespectful. But she claimed she was extremely religious and read the bible and bullshit like that. We'd even go to church, where I couldn't sit still for an hour and often times I had to leave mass early. For some reason though, I loved midnight Christmas Mass up at that big church in Mission Hill.

In the spring of 2012, we decided to take a vacation to Virginia Beach. We ended up taking my car to drive there. I was happy and content driving and listening to my cd mixes that I made for the trip. I listened to them over and over because of my OCD, and that got to her eventually. The worst behavior I had was my comfort go to show was 2 and a Half Men. I was obsessed with that show and watched it to help me go to sleep. Then when the seasons ended, I'd start again from the beginning, thus not allowing her to watch television. She got really upset about that and we'd fight. I honestly couldn't help it.

Back to the trip. We arrived at a nice hotel it was the Seaside or Seashell Hotel or some corny name like that. But the hotel was nice, it gave us a suite with a kitchenette and was spacious with a nice view of the ocean. I knew that Ann worked a lot, especially under the table for years, and I had no proof of how much money she'd bring home or home much she spent and how much she kept. Bottom line is, I was working at Harvard as well as Tillingers as a doorman, and wanted to give her a nice vacation.

When we first got there, immediately I got them Dairy Queen ice cream. Then we went to walk on the boardwalk, where we rented out bikes and could ride them on the boardwalk. We rented one of those 3 person bikes, and really enjoyed ourselves. We rode the whole boardwalk. It was a lot of fun. I entertained them and my hypomania kept me feeling too good and I'd crack them up by saying a lot of jokes and other funny sayings, a lot of it didn't make sense. It was like I was high on something, I just felt too damn good. The mania was a drug that kept me high, and I absolutely loved it.

The bad part came when I wanted to go out to a club. We ended up going out one night, where they had specials on vodka doubles and I was drinking many of those that night. I had a drinking problem and that was clear. It was like Pringles, once I started I couldn't stop! So, I was drinking having fun dancing with two Asian twins having the time of my life at first, while my wife sat in the corner. She told me that she was jealous of me dancing with other women, and I told her to calm down that I was just having fun! About 2 to 3 hours into the night, she began arguing with me about my drinking and I never liked when people talked about my bad drinking habit. I ended up spitting an ice cube in her face-but not on purpose I was just talking and expressing myself and somehow it shot out of my mouth and into her face. Right away she got mad and left me, all alone there in the club. This was a bad thing to do. I didn't know the area, it was like 1am at night, and I was all alone. Another big red flag with her. But of course I kept drinking, until I threw up on the floor. I felt it coming up more and went to the bathroom and threw up all over the toilet seat. As I walked out of the bathroom, 2 bouncers grabbed me and dragged me out of the club (wasn't the first time). I told them that I needed to get back my id. They left me outside while they went back to get it for me. Somehow, I was always one with the people, which Is weird because most of my life I felt like an outsider looking in. But when I needed help the good news was that I knew how to ask for it and so as I was walking I made friends with a group of guys around my age and they walked me home. Another time when we went to Miami Beach, I went to a club alone (the only time in my life that I went alone) and got drunk. I was very far from my hotel at like 2am, and I asked a bus driver if she was going to my hotel and she said she wasn't, but since it was 2am she said hop on I'll take you to your hotel. I realized that she saved me. Anything could've happened I could've gotten robbed, jumped, or arrested. But that night I recognized that bus driver as my angel-she protected me until I got to my hotel. I thanked her and was very grateful that a stranger had helped me. She didn't have to go out of her way to do that.

Back in Virginia Beach, the group of guys walked me to my hotel and I thanked them. This is one thing that I really noticed is that God has always protected me from anything. It's crazy how God is there for you when you least expect it. I'm not a religious person by any means, but do believe in a higher spirit.

At first, the guy at the door wouldn't let me in because I was drunk off my ass and he didn't believe that I had stayed there or had a room there. But eventually someone recognized me and confirmed that I had stayed there, and so that jackass let me in. When I got into my hotel room, Ann and her son were in a bed sleeping, and of course I woke them up. I\ was livid. How could Ann just abandon me when I needed her most!? What's worse, she turned off her phone so that I couldn't contact her. I finally fell asleep and ended up shitting all over the comforter. The hotel ended up charging me for it but they had every right too. They had to throw out the sheets pillows and comforter. The next morning we were driving back to Boston, and I was extremely hungover. I usually don't even get hungover, but this time I was very sick and felt nauseous. As I was driving, I pulled over by the bridge and threw up on the side of the road. I told Ann that she had to drive us because I couldn't. Problem was that she didn't even have her license, but she drove fine. By the way, it's important to note that I helped Ann a lot in life, I'll rant about that more later, but for now just know that I was the one that taught her to drive, that let her drive my car and helped her get her license. She drove for a few hours while I nursed my hangover. This event was another major red flag in the relationship.

Bar Hopping in NYC

In 2011 my parents and brother and I went to New York to visit my grandmother. My brother and I stayed there as well as my parents. My brother and I decided to go out one night to a Columbia University Bar. We went there with the intentions of hitting on girls and bringing one home. I was never good at talking to girls, in fact, my brother did better than me. I attracted girls whenever I was hypomanic, only then could I use my humor and high energy to intrigue women. It definitely worked, but all my life I felt like I was two different people. That's the problem with Bipolar. You know that when you're overconfident and charming that it's not the real you, in fact-you hate the real you because you're nothing like hypomanic Jan at that point.

So anyway, as I was saying, my brother and I go into this bar, and I did try talking to some girls they were nice, another one that I was macking along with my brother started getting annoyed with me. Now my thing is, as I've already mentioned before, drinking is my coping mechanism: it alleviates anxiety and helps me relax around crowds. Anyway, long story short we meet this one girl, and she's not interested in me. And by this time I am drunk and so I began to take a lighter out and play with it, and I start lighting her hair on fire and the smoke comes out of her hair! She turns around and says to me in a panic "What are you doing?" So we leave the bar.

Next, I am absolutely obliterated and have to pee. So we go to Duane Reade on Broadway and walk into the cooler isles, where I whip out my penis and start peeing in the cooler aisle. When I'm done, I zip up my pants and my brother is clearly distraught as he just saw me do this. As we try to walk out, a security guard stops us and asks me for my ID, or that he'll have to report this to the police. My brother tries to explain that I am bipolar, but I knew this tough guy rent a cop wasn't having it. So I ran out of the store and began running towards Riverside Drive. It was crazy how fast they called the cops, because I saw the flashing lights come seconds after I ran out, and so I quickly hopped into a taxi cab, and had it drive me to I believe 72st, where I entered the subway and called my brother and let him know to meet me in Times Square, which he did. When I got out of Times Square, it was snowing, but I felt more at peace. I felt bad that I peed at the drugstore, but there was no way that I was letting that guy have my ID. That was the end of that.

West Virginia-Bar Pop Champagne 2012

There was another time where my brother was working (he was an electrical engineer working contract jobs so every year or two his contract would be up and he'd move to different cities). Anyway, for this particular job, he lived somewhere in West Bumfuck in West Virginia. It was a small hick town with a very large population of low income hillbillies and lots of miners. So one night, we leave his apartment while my parents stay inside to go to the local bar. We begin drinking as usual, and we're doing shots of tequila and beers and then my brother says to me, "Yo you see those girls over there, let's talk to them." I said that I was good, and that I'd stay right here. So he went over, talked to them. The thing is, he had no game he was just like, "hey how you doing? You guys live around here?" I sat back with my beer, and enjoyed the show as the girls politely shot him down. My brother came back to the table, and in a few minutes the DJ played "Pop Champagne." Now you have to understand I LOVED hip hop. It absolutely fueled me and being that the artist Jim Jones was from Harlem, It made me love it even more. So I jumped up as soon as the song began to play and walked up to where those same girls who shot my brother down were dancing and began dancing with them. They noticed how much into the song I was and they grinded on me and later when I got back to my table, my brother told me that he couldn't believe that I did that! It was one of those moments were I felt proud to get my brother's respect and was proud that I danced with those girls. You see, music is my ultimate drug of choice-it gets me so pumped that I lose my anxiety and just become one with the music, and that's exactly what happened last night.

After we leave the bar, my brother is drunk, and one of the patrons at the bar calls and reports us for drunk driving. And so we made it to just outside of our home when we get pulled over by 2 cruisers. Then I look behind and there are 5 more cruisers (it's a small town, and it was evident that these guys had nothing better to do). So the cops come and start questioning my brother, and I'm in the backseat and begin to laugh hysterically and yell at the cop. Thank god the cops didn't do anything to me, but for my brother they made him walk a straight line and I couldn't stop laughing! My poor parents were looking outside from my brother's apartment in horror as the cops are making him walk a straight line. Thankfully, they didn't do anything to my brother but we were all fucking drunk and went home and straight to sleep.

2012 Vegas Trip

In May of 2012, I was invited to Vegas by an old acquaintance named Don who was the President of Men Integrated In Brotherhood for BSC back in 2002 and I was part of this club. It was a club that brought men of color together and kind of mentors and supports them throughout their college years. This is how I met Charles, Stan, and Don among others.

Anyway, Don and I were talking online when he invited me with the guys to go to Vegas for Memorial Day 2012. I decided to go, but it was a painful trip. You see, all that Don and the others wanted to do was to sleep with as many women as possible. They thought it was the cool thing to do. And I'll be honest, I wasn't impressed. Don brought hyennas back to the hotel. They were in a room at the MGM Grand. I'd never been there, and it was really nice to stay there, only I didn't get a bed, I had to sleep on the floor the first night. The next night, they finally brought up a cot for me but that was only because I called and was persistent in requesting one.

One night, we go club hopping. Stan of course meets two women from Montana. One of them was blonde and the other a brunette. He introduces me to them and they instantly begin to like me. I posed for pictures with them, but I guess it was a combination of shyness and morals. Although I wanted to take the brunette home and I know that I easily could have, my morals came into play, and I just couldn't muster up the courage to just fuck them as a one-night stand. Don saw this weakness, and he capped on me for it. The guy was a complete loser and we couldn't see eye to eye. They ended up taking the girls back to the hotel and fucking them, running a train on them, and I kind of felt bad because I didn't take the initiative to be like, "Hey let's go back to my hotel for some hot sex!" Nope didn't say any of that, and I stayed at the club getting absolutely obliterated drunk and watching Jermaine Dupri perform his hits that night. At one point I made eye contact with him, and he looked at me just drunk against the wall. He didn't say anything but I was totally wasted. When I walked back through the casino and back to the hotel a few hours later, I saw Stan with the blonde girl walking her back to the hotel. They said hi, and continued walking. The blonde girl looked at me and I pictured her thinking, "what a loser, this guy had the chance to fuck my friend and I and he backed out." Anyway, I passed out in the hotel room.

Another night we were out and I came in early because I was sleep deprived and wanted nothing more than to pass out in my cot. Don brings home another hyena overweight girl and he's fucking her as I walk into the room. She then gets up, walks over to put her clothes on, and I'm thinking would she let me fuck her. Maybe she would, hell this was Vegas, but I saw her as a person and didn't want to take advantage of her like Don did.

The thing is, I do have some sort of morals deep down. I respect women, and don't want to use them like that, but at the same time I get hypersexual and have one-night stands with women that I either meet out or on an online dating site.

The next day Don flipped out on me because I was locked out and called them and told them to come back and open the door for me, because of course I didn't have the key. He yelled at me over the phone and I couldn't take it. He was extremely arrogant and he stepped up to me and I didn't say anything back. And I actually regretted not hitting him or replying to his arrogant comments for years. He moved to Vegas a year later or so, but If I ever saw him again there'd be no friendly talk, I would walk up to him and beat the shit out of him because of how low he made me feel. That's not what friends do. Then again he never was a friend.

On Memorial Day I was going to take my flight home, and Don and the other idiot that was with him that I didn't know, made fun of me, they were like, "Why would you leave on Memorial Day this is when the action happens!" His friend was also pretty rude to me saying, "Why are you still here?!" The words hurt, and I made a promise to myself that I would hang out with people that didn't have my back. I took the red eye flight back to Boston.

BOSTON LIFE

Back in Boston I had just gotten a Prius and one Friday night some drunk teens opened my door. I jumped out of the car immediately and yelled, "Why would you do that?!" One of the kids swung at me but missed. They walked up to me and were about to do whatever they had to do to me. There was a big butch girl who said, "Damn, you a big nigga, huh?" I replied why yes, thank you. They were closing in on me, when one of the guys from the gangbanger house pulled up in his silver Nissan, and shouted to them to leave me alone. He said, "Eyo leave him alone, he's cool he's cool." And for some reason they instantaneously listened to him and walked away. I'm pretty sure this kid saved my life, because I could've been beat up and what's worse, in our neighborhood most teens were part of gangs and were carrying, and they could easily have shot me.

Back at work at the Harvard Dental Center, things were getting better with Clara and Tisha, but it was at this point where I became extremely depressed. You see, I started thinking and then overthinking to the point where I questioned my existence. I felt suicidal but never acted on it. Truth is, the work I was doing was office work and was boring as hell, and I felt that this wasn't the right job for me. The depression was kicking my ass, and so I took 2 weeks off to go to an outpatient program at Arbour Hospital in Jamaica Plain, where another psychiatrist put me on Wellbutrin and that was to help me stop the suicidal thoughts and it did-not only did it do that, it helped me to lose a little weight and that was always a good thing! But I do have to tell you, that getting help, especially at an inpatient/outpatient hospital is always great for your mental health, reason being that they offer individualized and group therapy, especially the group therapy helped me as I met some very cool people and also people that I could relate to. After 2 weeks, I went back to Harvard, feeling much better.

Ann panicked because she thought she was going to lose money since I wasn't working, but I had to do what I had to do. Also after I got out from the hospital, her uncle Albert put up a very small wooden front porch that he had his buddies build, and charged almost $5000 for it! When I found out from others that the job should've cost around $1500 I was livid with him. The stupid deck started calling apart because of poor workmanship and I was upset with Ann for hiring him. Next, were the windows. This son of a bitch wanted to install Harvey windows which were extremely expensive! I was like, fuck you we don't need these type of windows, and spent about$3,500 at Home Depot and had professionals install 6 windows for us.

Later on, her other Uncle Martin, who was much more humble and honest, helped us to transform our backyard that was overgrown with weeds, into a beautiful 2 car garage. He charged us very little, and so we had a bulldozer lay down asphalt and we also helped Uncle Martin with Quickrete Cement bags for the white vinyl fence that we put all around our property. For the first time in my life, I was extremely proud of my house, because it looked great! SWAT cars and other Boston Police stopped by to talk to us about our project, they loved it. FYI, anytime you make improvements to your home, you are also improving your community, and hence, the economic value of your property as well as surrounding houses in the community go up instantly.

At work we got a new supervisor, a Haitian lady with a big fucking attitude that I hated. I felt that she didn't know what was going on and yet judged me the harshest. Sometime in March, I got a letter from her that stated that I had excessive absences, kept incorrectly setting appointments, and other bullshit like that. She said that if I didn't improve it would lead to termination. I immediately called my union rep and asked what we could do? Truth was, I hated the environment, hated the work and felt like my calling was to be in a caring profession, such as a social worker or a nurse. I got into an argument with her when she began yelling at me, and so I wrote Catherine Lane, the Director an email stating that I just got yelled at. Then she retaliated stating that she never yelled at me. This email was one of the best ways to get upper management to begin to track her erroneous and erratic behavior because about a year later I found out that she had gotten fired for being too confrontational. The truth is, if you don't respect or like your manager/supervisor, or are working in a toxic environment, then leave your job to get a better new one. Your happiness is most important and if you see that you are in a hostile environment just leave your job.

What ended up happening was I began working with the union. My supervisor wanted to fire me, that was clear, but I wouldn't let her. I, along with the union worked out a deal with Harvard University to allow me to resign and collect my severance pay with continued benefits, as well as to go on unemployment. So in January 2013, I was gone from HSDM, with no work.

During this time I didn't know what to do, because I had felt extremely doubtful about myself. This was because I had problems with my attention and seemed like I kept fucking things up. The definition of someone who was insane was someone who A) Couldn't keep a job and B) Had difficulty maintaining social relationships. That was me. I had few friends, and at this point my mother and father (especially my father) convinced me to go on disability. It was the worst mistake ever, because when you're on disability nobody cares about you and you are poor for the whole time. Anyway, we went to a lawyer, got proof from medical documents from psychiatrists/psychologists spent a lot of time filing for this, and at first, we got denied. So, we appealed it and finally in October of 2013, I was approved for disability getting $1300 a month which was nothing. At the beginning when I had the SSDI, I was very unhappy. I gained weight from laying in bed literally most of the day, I stayed up watching Jimmy Kimmel and shit like that. I was depressed. And so, I got a part time job as a concierge.

This job was great, because I worked there since 2010. I was supposed to be a concierge but I was so nervous that they gave me the position of the doorman. I absolutely loved it! I worked at the Regatta, which were two towers of luxury condominiums. It was great the best parts were the clients, who really took care of us, especially around Christmas. Around August when people were moving in, we'd help them by reserving an elevator and opening the loading docks for them and helped them move their things in. They would tip us big. But the best part was Christmas when everyone was extra cheerful, I would work with Bill Brennan, who was the toughest guy I ever seen! Bill was a former boxer and legend had it that he walked out of Stardust Casino in the early 90s with $100k in cash and was never found. He knew so much about the mobsters and Las Vegas history and loved books on bank heists. He even knew Henry Hill who was played by Robert Deniro in Goodfellas and was friends with him in real life! Bill was very unique in that he'd get angry and wasn't afraid to tell someone off. I remember we had a bunch of people from like Columbia and other South American countries- these people were filthy rich, dressed in Gucci, especially the women, and studied business at schools like Bentley College and Babson. They drove very expensive cars like the Audi R8. The women looked absolutely gorgeous on Friday and Saturday nights when they'd wait in the lobby for the taxi or Uber to pick them up. Anyway, one day there was this spoiled rich girl, who wanted to use our phone. Bill allowed her but only said for 5 minutes, since we couldn't have the phones tied up. But this girl was on the phone for 10 plus minutes, and so Bill being Bill disconnected the line and demanded the phone back. Both the girl and I were in shock that he did this, but it took so much balls I had to tell him. Bill and I became good friends, and to this day I wonder how he's doing. He knew about my dark past. You see the truth was, I couldn't man the desk because I had panic disorder, and I didn't like crowds congregating at the lobby because I would panic. It wasn't a very good situation.

Another time a rich girl lost her expensive diamond ring in the trash chute, and she begged us to dig through the trash to find it. I wasn't going to do that, I said that's not my job, but the maintenance guy, Ronaldo did. He spent hours digging through the dumpster and after a few hours, he found the ring. He got a measly $100 for finding it.

It was a great job. We had the keys to the theater room and also the party room, I was invited to parties where I'd have a beer or two and sometimes if it was a big party they'd save food for us and even beers to take home! One of my best memories was when someone was throwing out a large screen Samsung TV, and they gave it to me for free. But I lie, this wasn't my best memory, it was the clients-I LOVED the community, and interacting with them as well as making connections with all the delivery drivers and taxi cab drivers. I met some real cool people who were students-important sons of politicians and oil owners in Saudi Arabia, who drove fancy cars and would sometimes even let me drive them! It was a great time working there, until I eventually left in 2014 for being bullied into working a double shift. I wrote a nasty letter to HR because I was livid at that manager and gave them 2 weeks notice. They however, terminated me immediately. It looked like I did something wrong and made the company look good, rather than correct the situation. Fuck them.

GRAD SCHOOL 2015

In August of 2015, I received a letter stating that I had been accepted into the Salem State University's Masters of Social Work program. I was thrilled to hear this! I would go twice a week on a part time basis, and I absolutely loved learning! I'm one of those people, who soaks up knowledge like a sponge, and if college was free I'd spent my life studying-I love it!

In September I began taking my first semester, it was social policy and Human Development, both of the classes I really loved. I did very well for my first term, straight A's in both classes, and in December Ann, my stepson and I went to Trinidad for 2 weeks. I felt neglected by Ann. She left me in my room for two weeks to watch tv while she socialized and cooked with her odd family. She never showed me around nor did anything, and when I spoke to her family, especially her mother, I sensed a coldness almost which led me to conclude that she didn't really approve of me or like me. We had nothing in common. Actually my favorite person in her family was Larry, Ann's disabled younger brother who was in a wheelchair and very sick. He was a natural healer, who helped me when I got a toe infection and had to go to the emergency room at MGH to get it removed. Anyway, I turned manic and would stay up nights in Trinidad writing. I applied for several scholarships and wrote on life in the hood. Carlos was an inspiration to me, and the hood was like a separate part of the country that the outside world never knew much about, and ignored, while there was lots of black on black violence and people dying every single day. I wrote about misguided youths and how they had access to illegal firearms with scratched out serial numbers. I wrote about Carlos, and how his father was an alcoholic and he had no guidance in his life. I ended up being selected for the Daniel Aaron Collins Scholarship in 2016, which gave me $500 for school. It wasn't about the money, it was about the fact that my writing was so influential to a lot of people, and I ended up with a plaque on the wall with my name in it. I went to a honorary dinner where I got awarded the scholarship. It was in Salem and both my parents came, as well as Ann and her son. Anyway, I remember I had a huge panic attack and had a hard time so bad that I didn't even eat! I finally accepted an award and walked quickly back to my seat, but before that was interrupted by my father who wanted to desperately take a picture with me and my award, but I didn't want to. The lady who presented me with the award, called me over and made me basically stop to take a picture in front of all the people who sat down and looked at me, making me feel uncomfortable. But I quickly took the picture and was upset that my father embarrassed me like that. I went back to my seat. The presenter told the audience that for Thanksgiving every year we would help the homeless by passing out turkey dinners that we cooked every year and passed them out in Boston Common and Downtown Crossing.

I met some friends at Salem State but one of my problems, especially in the second year, was that I felt inferior in my classes, and before class I'd do anything I could to relieve the anxiety, from taking CBD oil to eating a few bananas which I heard relieves anxiety attacks. They helped somewhat but it wasn't the end all cure all.

I had one friend in my class and that was Jenn, and even she backstabbed me in the end because she didn't believe that I should be there, and she wouldn't give me a reference when I asked for a job.

MASTER SPLINTER AND HIS FRIENDS 2015-2017

In 2015, another building next door was built and they had one dumpster for all the tenants. Well, this brought by a rat infestation. I remember that there were rats and mice even on our bed! We saw all the feces and it was clear they were rummaging from the other building through tiny holes and into our kitchen, basement, and even our bedrooms! It got to the point where the rats would find shelter inside of my Lexus RX350 because it was warm for them in the winter. So when I opened up the hood one day, not only were there multiple rat droppings all over the engine but all of my wires were chewed up by the rats! I had to get my car repaired because of this. I read everything about getting rid of them. The internet had suggested moth balls and we tried that, although we found out that the smell gives cancer so it wasn't healthy to put them in under the hood anymore. I got some electronic device that was supposed to scare rats away, and that did help to a degree I must say. But still, the problems persisted. I ended up spending a lot of money of rat traps and rat bait and hired an exterminator who helped me set up traps outside by the fence. It finally started working I would find multiple dead rats the size of footballs by the fence. The gross thing was, I had to physically pick them up with my hands. They felt stiff and cold, and it scared the shit out of me! Eventually though we called the management company and told them that if they didn't do something about the rat problem that we would have to talk to a lawyer. They immediately hired an exterminator on their end.

I got a cat also for the rats but he wasn't a good cat-he would go behind the walls and instead of shitting in his litter box he kept shitting behind the wall! The other problem was we didn't have heat down in the basement and it wasn't insulated as well. I had a good friend named Tony help me insulate the whole basement. He even had to cut a hole in the wall and that's where we found out about the cat shit. He brought over his huge vacuum cleaner and we cleaned all the shit within the walls. I'll be honest, I couldn't have done this without Tony's help he played a big part in lowering my heating bills-I was already a resourceful person and working with Boston's ABCD program to get funding for paying some of my heating costs, but it wasn't easy. Tony helped me cut my bill down by 30%. It used to be $6-700 per month on heating costs alone. I found these great energy efficient baseboard heaters that Tony put in for me. He saved me by insulating the basement and installing all of the baseboard heaters. He was a good man. And the way I knew him was because I worked as a caregiver in Quincy for his teenage son with Autism, James and he was my boss.

Being on disability was difficult because it didn't pay much per month, and so I would have to get jobs all under the table as a caregiver. I worked with some amazing people and I don't want to give away their names. I worked in Quincy, Waltham, and Canton to name some of my client's homes. I learned so much about Autism, and was very passionate about helping those with autism, I actually became an ABA therapist for about a year. The work was great-it was rewarding to help clients achieve independence by reinforcing positive behavior and punishing negative behaviors.

The point was, that living on disability kept me poor, and by me working under the table I was bringing an additional 1500 to 2000 per month in addition to my disability. I was balling and nobody even knew it. School was hard in the sense that the first question that everyone asks you what you do for work, and so I'd hide at first the fact that I was disabled and told them I work as a caregiver with teens with autism.

December 2016

So I had this friend, Terell who I thought was my best friend at the time but I was wrong. I'll tell you later what happened. But I'd like to tell you guys one of my worst manic episodes that I've ever lived to tell. It started with one cold Saturday night in December of 2016, when I was getting ready to meet Terell and his friends at Venu nightclub in Boston. I dressed up in a royal blue Calvin Klein shirt topped with a nice suit jacket and jeans. I felt good. As I was about to enter my car and leave, I noticed this couple had parked their car right in front of my garage, blocking me from exiting and being on my way. I waited while they were in the store, and when he came out I lost my temper and flipped out on him. As I was screaming and approaching him I intimidated him and I liked that feeling of control and power that I had over him. He apologized, and him and his wife left immediately. So that was what triggered me first.

When I arrived at Venu, I met up with Terell and his fiancé, and another girl who was this cute shorty that was Puerto Rican with a beautiful body. Well, she was into me, and I could've easily went home with her that night, but I fucked up everything because I couldn't stop drinking the entire night. I must've had like 20 vodkas with Redbull it was terrible. At one point some guy said something to me I don't remember what but it was something along the lines of don't you love yourself? And that meant a lot to me because someone was paying attention and so I gave him a hug and teared up. The guy was absolutely right, and I'm pretty sure he was a counselor or something.

Anyway, back to the Puerto Rican fly shorty. She was beautiful, and I asked if I could buy her a drink, she replied sure. As we went to the bartender and they fixed her a drink, I realized that I couldn't pay for the drink and the bartender was a complete bitch. She demanded we pay for the drink only problem was there were like 4 different bars at Venu and I didn't know with which bartender I left my card on tab with! My friend ended up paying for the drink and she wasn't too thrilled about it. I told her I'd pay her back as soon as possible.

Anyway, I blew my shot with her and continued to chug shots like they were Gatorade. At one point in the night I remember telling her that I couldn't stop drinking, and she said switch to water. She was a friend, and I really liked her she was real, but not even she could save me.

At the end of the night at 2am, I started hitting on girls saying, "Hi I'm Jan and I have full dental!" It got a lot of girls laughing, and in particular this one upscale blonde girl that wanted to go fuck. She asked where we would go and I honestly was such a drunken mess and told her that we could go to some made up bar in Dorchester. When she noticed that I was drunk she immediately left. That kind of hurt because them rejecting me had nothing to do with my looks but had everything to do with my consumption of too much alcohol!

On the way home I ended up driving my own car and I had a 6 pack of beer in the car and continued drinking bottles of Yuengling and throwing them out of my window as I was driving down the Zakim Bridge. I honestly wanted a state trooper to pull me over and get arrested. I needed someone to notice me, and I wanted help. I was a raging alcoholic and needed help.

When I got home, I undressed and was in my blue shirt and orange boxers. I had a major manic episode and went outside and began screaming "Carlos is the Truth!!! Fuck all of ya'll!! I am the truth!" And threw beer bottles outside onto the streets. The streets were definitely watching but at first kept quiet. Ann tried to stop me from doing this, but I remember I knocked over some shit in the bathroom cabinet and ended up pushing Ann. I kept going back outside and yelling, "I AM THE TRUTH." And cussing and all of that. Then I went home and cried very loud in my bed very loudly. I actually thank my community because they could've easily called the Boston Police and I could've been easily shot because knowing myself I would've been violent. So thank you streets, you saved me. Later on when I woke up around 4am to some gangster yelling at me. He wanted to come outside and fight me because he said something along the lines of "You're a bitch ass we have real niggas dying here everyday!!" But I didn't come out, I was very afraid. The next day I thought this was pretty nice of the gang bangers, but they all put out empty bottles of liquor in front of my house. Not sure why they did that, maybe to pay a tribute to me, or maybe perhaps because they sympathized with my condition. All I know is that I needed to change and that was clear.

On another note, Ann was going back to school to become a medical assistant. I was actually the one who helped her enroll in school and applied for her and did everything else. The plan was that she'd graduate school and find a job in the medical field, and we'd save up to get out of Boston. But I began to grow very distant from her. She wasn't a well woman, she was broken, she flipped out and had tantrums all the time, and I felt like I wasn't loved anymore and was neglected. And so, I did the worst thing possible...went on Match and Tinder. There were a handful of women that after one date I took them back to the condo and fucked their brains out... just to prove to myself that I could.

One was a Dominican girl that I met online, we messed around in my Lexus RX350 in the back seat as we took breaks smoking good high quality Indica weed. Her name was Wally, and I was extremely attracted to her. She sat on top of me and I felt her, she was soaking wet, but still didn't let me fuck her. I stayed friends with her for about 2 years and every time I went to her house she teased me my dancing and grinding on me, or getting on top of me in the bedroom and "riding me" with our clothes on. I really liked her, its too bad that she moved on from me after I pissed her off. The reason that I pissed her off was because I called her out on her bullshit. She was just a tease, she knew I wanted her and she played with me, and so I told her that and she got upset. So that relationship was never mended.

I met several girls who were in school for nursing-these women were LOTS of fun in bed, and one girl was a Latina who was a U.S. Marine, I hooked up with her as well after drinking at Dave and Busters in Woburn.

I was all over the place with women but my favorite girl, was this thick Vietnamese girl I met on Tinder. I told her right away that I wanted to eat her til she exploded. She made arrangements for me to pick her up right away and bring her to a hotel. The first time I went to a cheap motel in Braintree, like a Hotel 6 or something. I kid you not, we fucked for 5 hours, with a break to McDonalds where she got an ice cream cone. This girl was smoking and absolutely the best lay of my life. She had purple dyed hair, was thick in all the right places, and knew how to fuck very well. She had tattoos all on her side of her stomach going down her thigh, and it was very hot. As I said, we spent all night fucking, I don't even think I've done that before up until now, all I can say is, it was hot and the best ever for me! Not every man and woman are physically compatible, but I found my match. I could bend her in all sorts of crazy positions and enter her vagina from the back. The best was doggystyle though, she had an amazingly thick ass. Well, this girl liked me, and we had another hookup, a few weeks later, but this time, It was at a fancy hotel in downtown Boston and she invited me. Again, I brought alcohol because I was trying to kill or numb the pain. I couldn't understand it and neither could she. I fucked her but couldn't come, and so I took a walk and she texted me to come back. I texted her back asking her if she could make me come. She replied yes. I don't know what it was about that text message, but it turned me on. I went back there and fucked her as she was in her black laced lingerie from Victoria's Secret. I fucked her until I came hard.

One of my problems, however, was that I would fuck without a condom and soon had to be tested for Syphilis and other STDs. All these girls I was extremely irresponsible and careless with, and I know I needed to be more careful. But I hated condoms. At MGH, I told the doctor that it hurt when I peed, and she gave me a shot for HIV, but luckily, I didn't end up having any STDs.

Things got worse when Anne's stepson began noticing that I would be bringing women home, and he did what any little boy who didn't understand the man code would do, he'd tell his mother. When she confronted me about it I told her it was true, and that we had disconnected, and things had forever changed. She cried hard, and ever since we moved to Weymouth and me cheating on her happened, she couldn't forgive me. She hated her life, hated the fact that she worked almost an hour and a half away, hated that I bought the condo without her permission. She made up whatever she could, but the truth was, she wanted the condo just as much as I did. But our relationship was going nowhere fast. Next, her brother Larry died. The one that I really liked, and she accused me for not "being there for her" in her time of need. But that was bullshit, I did all I could to comfort her, only I always didn't know what to say when a friend or family member died, and so I just told her that I was very sorry for her loss. My mother I remember was extremely insensitive to her brother's death and said that she should get over it, that people die all the time it's a part of life.

Things between us were getting worse, and there was a lot of tension every time that we were in the same room together, it just wasn't healthy. I want the world to know that I did everything for this woman. I taught her to drive, got her green card, got her enrolled in school and then created a resume for her and applied to all the places because she didn't know how. Her son was the worst, laziest person I'd ever met in my life, and I abhorred him. Didn't like him at all. He was failing in school and Ann wanted to get him into St Joseph's, which was a private Catholic school in Brighton. I was very much opposed to this, but she did what she wanted. I found out that shed save money because she made me pay the condo fee which was like $400 a month, and in the meantime she'd pay for his tuition which was about $600. I remember she begged me to write essays to get him into BC High or other schools, and I did. I did everything for him and I shouldn't have. He had to want it. There was no ambition, no desire, there was none of that. He was just there, playing on his Playstation for hours and hours and giving me a high heating bill during the winter months because he turned up the heat all the way up to 80 degrees. It was bullshit, I even spoke to him about not setting the thermostat more than 68 degrees, but he didn't listen, nor care. It was me who did everything for that kid. Ann felt guilty because he felt she neglected him. She blamed me. It wasn't my fault it was her own fault for working to the point where she never got to see him. I gave him rides to his job at McDonalds and I was the one who got him to his prom when he had no rides. When she did spend time with her son, she resorted to cooking or watching her stupid cooking shows on Food Network or the Hallmark Channel. Man I hated the Hallmark channel, she watched corny ass Christmas movies all year long. You know, those extremely cheesy movies about Santa and finding love during the holiday season? Yup that was her. My point is though, that she was broken, and she didn't know how to love her son. It was never my fault all though she accused me all the time and placed the blame on me. She said I took up all her time. Fuck her though. It was her responsibility to care for her son and she didn't do that. I was tired of being blamed for her own wrong doings.

She didn't trust me anymore, and now she resented me as well. It felt like she was a timed bomb, just waiting to explode at any minute, which she did, many times. This is why I never wanted to marry again; because she was an emotional wreck and would cry and whine to me, and I honestly couldn't take it. It wasn't good for my mental health.

Finally, one day we went to pick up her son from McDonalds at his part time job. I had just eaten a fine marijuana infused brownie, and I couldn't drive back due to me being extremely high. I asked her to drive and she got really mad, she told me in the car, "Jan, I want a divorce." It hit me right in the heart like a sharp dagger, but

I didn't argue with her. I hated her as well, and I wanted to be out of this as soon as possible.

The next two months was hard, as we lived together but slept in separate bedrooms. She made me buy all my bedroom furniture dresser and nightstand when she could've easily shared hers. Finally, in September, she did everything she could to make me leave the house. She knew I was dating Erika, a fun, down to Earth girl I had just met on match, and she despised me for it and would stop at nothing to make my life a living hell. It started when she tore down my shower curtains so I couldn't shower. She got in my face a couple of times and I almost lost my temper, but I'd never forget what my parents told me. That as angry as she made me, if I so much as laid a finger on her I'd get arrested, and I didn't want that so I took deep breaths as she threw my jackets on me and yelled to her son, "Get this man out of MY house!!" She was a real bitch, I should've never married her, especially since there were red flags early on in the relationship. But I did what she wanted and moved out.

She was an angry and spiteful woman. When I was finally out of the house, she then suspended my cell phone service, and because of her, important job contacts couldn't reach me and Erika would have to give me her phone just so that I could speak to my friends and family.

SSU 2016 and Field Education Dept/Internship/CSR

Although I didn't really begin to struggle with the panic attacks and agoraphobia til the second year of Salem State, I was an A student and had been awarded the Daniel Aaron Collins Scholarship, The coolest part about it, was that my name was on a plaque on the wall for all to see. I felt very proud of this. I remember we were in Trinidad, and I was manic, and of course I would wake up every morning when the Rooster would crow at 3:30 in the morning. That was actually my favorite part of the trip, the fact that I could stay up outside at night and type on my computer. So I wrote a couple of essays to apply for scholarships. I wrote about what I knew-the hood life during those times. Although living in Roxbury scared me because of all that I saw there, at the same time, it inspired me, to want to help youth offenders through my career as a social worker. The young men such as Carlos who was in the Bloods gang and had worn an ankle bracelet, those were the type of people that I wanted to help. I felt that if we had more mental health resources in disenfranchised places such as Roxbury, we could help keep the kids off of the streets. It's those inner city vulnerable populations that needed the help most-places that the upper classes of society ignored and looked down upon, instead of lending a helping hand. This is something that needs to be changed. We are all products of our environment, and in those environments youth offenders join gangs in order to get love, because often times there's no father figure present and there's a lot of peer pressure from other teens to do bad things to become accepted. There are a lot of mental health challenges in the hood, and its up to us to raise mental health awareness and provide more resources for mental health in inner city communities such as Roxbury.

Anyway, it came time for my internship. I was extremely excited to start. I had been interviewing and basically got any internship I wanted. But I wanted to intern at government/state agencies like DMH or the VA Hospital, but for some reason the powers that be were telling me that I couldn't do this. I was upset by this. They tried to suggest for me, and I didn't like that. So ultimately, I interviewed and decided to join the Children's Services of Roxbury-what a huge mistake that was. First of all, my supervisor, would be Donald, and he wasn't suited to be a manager or my supervisor. At the beginning, he didn't even have a plan for me, and so I'd be on the computer in the office just doing the required courses all day. He didn't even check on me, and I spent 12 hours in the site office one day! The person who found me was the Director of the program, who told me to go home and was shocked that Donald wasn't checking in on me. I hated Donald. I even provided documentation that said that I was disabled. At first, he threw lots of cases on me, but I informed him that I wanted to take it slower, so that I could learn everything. He interpreted as I didn't want the required amount of caseloads and then he'd later say that I didn't want to work. They had us in training all week and every Wednesday I'd have to go to a weekly meeting which of course had me anxious and uncomfortable. The trainings were led by idiots that were fresh out of jail and didn't know what they were doing. They wanted me to do a mock therapy session and when I had no idea what to do, the others were criticizing me and so I told them all, "I don't have to know this right now, I'm an intern, I'm here to learn this stuff!" This organization as a whole was so horrible. The management was terrible and I worked so fucking hard.

In school we'd meet once a month in this field ed group and had assignments and a lot of work to complete. I was very quiet and didn't speak up and if you're interested in social work grad school, I'll tell you one thing: There are many uppity white privileged white woman there who were terrible and shouldn't have pursued social work because how could they relate to what was going on out there? They couldn't and they had no idea how to handle things. Well, one day, this stupid girl, who I'll never forget said to me in front of everyone, "You don't ever talk, it's kind of scary." Then another girl told me, "Yea its really weird." I replied arrogantly and told them to mind your own business and that, she was entitled to her own opinion. But looking back, I should've told them bitches that I had a disability which was social anxiety. These people couldn't seem to understand that they were supposed to understand that people in grad school have all kinds of disabilities, and the fact that they would say that to me just justifies my beliefs that they didn't belong in social work graduate school. These types of people were exactly the type of people who unfortunately many times are social workers, and they do a horrible job but that's the reality of it, and this needs to change.

Anyway, Donald gave me a terrible review even though I busted my ass. He told my field liaison advisor, Rachael, that I kept to myself and didn't socialize with anyone-and this was untrue. I had so much online work to do that I was focused on completing it, but I did get to know a few good people.

My job was a family therapist, to use expressive art and play with kids who lived in the inner city. I was passionate about helping others and worked hard. I had 3 families to care for a week, and this was an internship so I was not getting paid. The only good thing about working at Children's Services of Roxbury was the fact that I lived like literally 2 blocks from there so I could walk there or park my car really close if I wanted to.

In the end, we came up with an action plan between my field site professor and Donald. In the action plan it basically stated that If I attended all meetings and internship meetings and worked really hard that this would help me pass for the last term. I did everything they told me to do, and at the end of the internship. Ronald failed me. He took me to a room and asked me very complex questions where I knew I would fail. When I couldn't answer one, he would humiliate me by laughing with his co- worker. Why the co-worker would be in the room I had no idea, but he was. I wasn't comfortable in there, and it was clear they wanted me to fail. I had no idea why, but they didn't like me, and didn't want to pass me. In the end he failed me by not giving me a passing grade of a '3'. He mostly gave me 2's. I wasn't surprised, but it hurt.

In a few weeks, Sue Goldman, the Field Ed Director called me up to set up a time to come in for a meeting. I showed up there alone, of course with anxiety and I didn't defend myself. I paid for all my books and was ready for my first day of class returning from the summer and along with Professor Blinderman, they told me that I didn't pass field and they wanted me to take a year off and focus on work that had a clinical aspect to it. All I did was shake Sue's hand and ignore the other lady. I thanked her not sure why and left the school in my Lexus RX350. I felt melancholy. I felt like a failure. That was September 2017, and I'd never forget the date.

I tried calling a lawyer and they asked for ADA paperwork from the Disabilities center to prove that I was discriminated against, and that's why I would be let go from the school, but the problem was, that when they filled out my accommodation paperwork, they did not include the reason for my accommodations, the fact that I had social anxiety disorder and bipolar. They only wrote the list of accommodations that I could have, but not my diagnosis. I was furious. I began thinking that they did this shit to me on purpose just in case I went to a lawyer...The lawyer said that without this documented that he could do nothing. And so, I didn't sue the school.

SEPT 2017-LEAVING SALEM STATE

School gave me a purpose, it gave me a chance to focus on something that I was passionate about, and I loved learning. I'm one of those people that is a lifelong learner, and so any type of classes will greatly benefit me if it's something that I'm curious and passionate and excited about.

A few weeks had passed after I left Salem State, and I began to drink heavily. My drink of choice was Gray Goose or Coconut Ciroc with a splash of green apple mix. From then, my drinking increased ten fold. I'd drink around 8-10 shots a day, 3x the amount that I was supposed to drink. Everywhere I went, restaurants or bars, I'd drink as a way to numb the pain. But truth be told, even before Salem State I would always drink to numb the pain. I felt like a failure, and from my past traumas I just couldn't put the bottle down, since the days of me dating Anette. I started thinking and then overthinking about all my failures that I discounted the positive. I didn't remember that I had a plaque on the wall winner of the 2016 Daniel Aaron Collins Scholarship, nope that didn't matter. I went to therapists but none of them could help me.

In February of 2018, that melancholy turned into anger and resentment. And so I did what any normal guy who's pissed off would do. I wrote Sue Goldman a nasty letter. In the letter I explained to her that I didn't fail, but rather she failed me. I went on in many pages how mentors are there to help you not give you the axe because you made a mistake. They wanted me to fail. Seemed like I was born to lose, built to win.

I gave up, and for the next 3 years I drank heavily to the point that my doctor would tell me that I have fatty liver, that my liver was scarred and liver enzymes were high and she was really worried about me and that I had to stop drinking. Both therapists and friends told me that it seemed like both the professor and the intern manager were at fault, and that I needed to learn from this failure and move on. It took me a while to realize this, eventually it would lead to Ann leaving me when I was high and told her she'd have to drive her son home from work, because I couldn't.

DIVORCE-APRIL 2019

For the last 3 months Ann and I had been fighting over money, and her true colors came out-she was a savage, and she wanted to milk me for everything that I had. It's crazy how when money is involved you see people for who they really are, not who they pretend to be. My father always told me that the number one problem in the world is money. When there's money around people become greedy and evil, and selfish, quick to backstab their own people just to have more. More on this later.

Anyway, Ann would try to milk me off of every penny. She would say that I owed her this for that, when I was already still paying my share of the rent, the whole condo fee so that her lazy stupid son could go to a private school and covering the cost of heat. It was me who signed up for Boston's ABCD, a non-for-profit organization downtown that helped folks cover a portion of the heat. Our heating bills were out of control, they were around $600-$700 dollars per month! I had enough of her bullshit. Why did I continue to pay my half of the rent and other bills if she kicked me out and I didn't even live there. That's when I decided to stop paying rent or anymore bills. I told her that I shouldn't have to pay if I don't live there, and she was livid. This is when she began to worry about being able to make the mortgage herself. She knew that this house needed to sell, before she could move to another house with the profits that she took with this house. So I did just that, I wrote her a letter explaining what I would do.

We had this mediator from my mother's job, a good friend of my moms, who was Director of some office at the Harvard Medical School. She volunteered to mediate our divorce and while I am thankful for her, she wasn't the greatest mediator because she feared Ann, and because of that she fucked up a few things. All the while though, I never told Ann that this lady worked with my mother because she wouldn't agree to this, instead, I told her that I found her online.

We agreed to split the profit of the house half half, even though it wasn't fair because a large chunk of the profit came from my first house that I sold-I transferred over 100k into the new mortgage on the condo. The profit of the Weymouth property was about 66k, and Ann was her usual hard headed self and wanted to ask for alimony. I told her that you couldn't take alimony from me, because I was on disability, and then she wanted child support, but her son wasn't my child. She even wanted me to sign papers that said I would be adopting her kid, but I refused to do so. She probably wanted to use that eventually to fuck me out of my money to pay for that boy who did nothing but play video games and raise the heat to the max. I basically told her that if she asked the Court for alimony that I would tell the court that she has been working under the table this whole time.

There was another thing. When we sold the first house, like 60k of it went to pay off her credit cards, loans, and auto loans. All that got paid off and it wasn't fair to split the profits 50/50. So I demanded that she pay me back my half which was like 30k, but she didn't want to. I told her that if she didn't cooperate that I would immediately hire a lawyer on my behalf (even though I had no money for a lawyer). This seemed to get her scared, and she began texting me to negotiate a price. I told her $15k, she wanted to give me $3k, which was complete bullshit. I told 10k, she went down to 7k and wouldn't budge. We ended up agreeing on 7k plus my half of the money that we had made in profit from selling the first home plus the appreciation of this condo. Truth be told, we only had the condo for about 2 years, and we didn't make much off of it, only about 8k.

So April 2019 came and of course if you've ever been to probate court you'd know it is very difficult to fill out the paperwork correctly. Once again, Ann didn't do shit so I did all the work for the paperwork. Every time I kept trying to turn it in, the clerk at the office would tell me something wasn't done right or I was missing something and they'd give it back to me. I had to redo it twice before the next time they finally accepted it, and we immediately got a court date.

On the day of court, I was extremely nervous, but I knew she was more nervous than me. Everyone reassured me that It was going to be ok. When the judge called us up she asked if we agree to divorce each other in an uncontested divorce, we answered yes. Before it was over, I asked the judge if in that paperwork it was written that Ann owed me the 7k, just to be sure. She said it was in there. I was thrilled about that, now she wouldn't try to back out. I made almost $40k from the sale of the our condo, and Ann bought a house but she wouldn't tell anyone where. I did some research and found out it was in Fitchburg.

For the record I just want to say that the way things ended was horrible. Her true colors showed me that she was fake as shit, and I wish her the best but she's a terrible person and I never want to see her again. I still resent her in a way for what she did to me. The way she treated me, and that is sad after all I did for her. She can choke on a dick for all I care, if anyone deserved it it's her. All I have to say is that karma catches up to you at one point or another, and so its important to do right and be good to everyone in your life. You'll get what's coming to you.

ERIKA

Erika was nice enough to let me stay in her studio with her, and I moved in with her in her Quincy studio in Quincy.

I loved the Wollaston section of Quincy it was one of the best places I had ever lived. The Asians were quiet and peaceful, and all was well with the world and I. I stayed with Erika for a year and a half. At first Erika had no clue that I was married but divorcing Ann, but when I told her she finally understood. Ann was a real bitch. One thing that she did that really pissed me off was she suspended my phone line since I was paying her every month. This really got me upset because I was unable to call back potential employers and my friends.

Anyway, Erika and I began dating and before you knew it, she was my new girlfriend. I started realizing what I'd been missing all this time. Erika was a fun girl with a great personality. and I told her I loved her after about a month of meeting her. She was fiercely loyal, and genuine, and she knew and liked the same music and pop culture and actors that I liked which I never had with Ann. Overall, she was exactly who I'd been looking for at first.

We spent every waking moment together, and in March we drove to New Hampshire to stay at a log cabin for a few days. All we did was have sex and lots of fun driving around, eating at diners. She was a great partner.

Like I mentioned, we lived in a tiny studio on a twin size bed at first, before I bought her a full size mattress. She cared so much for me in my life when it seemed like no one else did. She knew about my past traumas and my night terrors and hitting her in my sleep and knew that these traumas affected me still to this day. Erika at first seemed to be a perfect girl in my eyes; she was very nurturing and caring, just like my mother was to me. You know that saying you end up marrying your mother? Well its kind of true. As individuals we go through life looking for a partner with similar qualities.

Erika was great and I liked her instantly because she was Bipolar I, and we got along very well. On our first date, I took her to the 99 Restaurant in Quincy, and we talked for a while it seemed. We were there over an hour, just enjoying each others company, and I learned a lot about her and her illness. We seemed to have a lot in common, especially how the Bipolar took over our lives and how every day was a struggle to fight it. Erika said that her mood would go up and down, and that she was in psychiatric wards over 15 times in her life! I found that incredibly interesting and was immediately drawn to it.

I told her I loved her actually in the Weymouth condo, after only dating for like a month. She was really special to me. We would go out everywhere, we liked the same music, same taste in movies and even food, and she took me to New Hampshire to show me more about where she spent her summers as a child. I decided to pay for her to come with me to Las Vegas later on. The problem happened a few months into the relationship, I'd say at about the 6month mark, when Erika got into a depressed mood. I didn't know how to help her except just to be there for her. Now I rapid cycle, and I know how bad depression feels and could relate to Erika, but her depression was the worst that I had ever seen. When she was down, she was down. She couldn't function at all...she became agoraphobic, lethargic, spend hours just sleeping in her bed and ordering takeout all the time. She wore the same clothes for several days and didn't shower. I'd have to prompt her to take a nice shower. I'll be honest, the first time I saw her in this condition I began to cry, because I felt really bad because I didn't know how to help her.

We were in a committed relationship and I really loved her and cared for her, but the fact was that I couldn't handle her moods. And when she was depressed she got abusive toward me, saying some nasty things.

But Erika, if you're reading this, you've made me a better person. You were the person that I was looking for my whole life. I wanted someone that I could relate to, someone like you, who also suffered from Bipolar and could see my pain through her eyes. I felt all alone in this world without Erika, and she was my rock. I knew that I didn't see a future with her because she was messy, unorganized, but I knew that we'd be friends forever. Me and her, we were soulmates and nothing would tear us apart.

Erika cashed out her 401k, it was about 60k. Her parents assumed that I was using her, which I wasn't. She told me she wanted me to have nice things and would constantly pay for the finest hotels in Boston, and I was able to buy everything from clothing, shoes, and more. She even took out $20,000 and bought us a Tesla Model S. Now, nobody had ever done this for me before. It was clear that she cared and wanted to see me happy. She was genuine, she was the truth, she was my missing puzzle, but I knew deep down that I would never end up with her. The fact is, I wasn't taking advantage of her, at least I didn't mean to intentionally. Problem was that we were both very manic and when there's money I spend lavishly. Erika was okay when she was depressed but when she was manic she could be scary. One night she shaved her head and stood by me in my bed as I was sleeping. She kept waking me up when all I wanted to do was go to sleep. She was completely delusional, talking about how Leonardo DiCaprio was her soulmate and that she could read his mind. She was saying that we were vampires and would live forever among other things. The red flags in my mind went off, this wasn't good. I remember I called a handful of ambulances for her because of her mania and delusions. But the worst time was when she was manic and decided to meet me in Plymouth. She was supposed to come down to the Cape and took the train, only her phone battery died and I couldn't reach her. She sounded manic from her texts. I called my mother and asked for advice, she told me that I should drive to Plymouth and find her, and I did. She was walking around with a shaved head, bad makeup made up, walking around in my boxers no pants! I was literally both shocked and scared at the same time. Apparently she had been doing her laundry and then walked off, and was wandering all over town. I told her to get in the car and immediately called her mother. I told her mother to call the Plymouth Police and get medics out here. This was by far the worst state that I'd ever saw Erika in. So the police came, the ambulance came, and they took her away. Erika was in hospitals since her early 20s. She stayed at inpatient psych wards 15 times in her life. But I loved her, and I would always be there for her...she didn't want me to call the ambulance on her because she didn't think that anything was wrong with her, but everyone else could see that there was. She just needed help, and they took her to Beth Israel Plymouth Hospital that day.

PABLO AND NEPHEWS 2019

Christmas, 2019, my parents and I went to Mars, a suburb outside of Pittsburgh where we went to visit my brother in his newly constructed townhouse. It was the first time that I'd seen where he lived. The house was amazing. It had 3 floors was extremely spacious, with a brand new kitchen, jacuzzi upstairs, and a finished basement. I was very proud of my brother for all of his accomplishments, and I told him that. We started from the bottom with a dream, and he made it in life. He was rich, married with kids. It seemed like he had everything he wanted.

My nephews were absolutely adorable, they were 1 and 3 when I came to visit him. Jason was the eldest, and Carter was the youngest. We had a great time at Christmas, and what made it great was seeing how awesome my father was with the kids. He'd pretend to be a penguin hopping around with a ball in between his legs and make all kinds of funny noises-the children absolutely adored him! I began to see a different side of him. For the first time in my life, I saw him very happy and free, free from whatever was chaining him inside. I asked my father how he was so good with kids, and he told me that he watched like 9 children in his family when he was young. I was really impressed and it was hard but the man that had abused me all my life I began to have mercy on him, as I realized that it wasn't his fault-one day he told us the story about his life in Ecuador.

HEART OF GOLD, TROUBLED MIND

My father's mother left both my father and my grandfather at an early age, when he was just a boy, to go live in New York City. A big part of the problem was that my father didn't have that love from a mother figure. His father owned a clothing store and he would tailor there, and worked very long hours and my father barely saw his father. He credits his grandmother as his hero, since she was the one that taught him everything and raised him at a young age.

My father lived in a building with other members of family, and as a young boy and teenager, he'd fear for his life as his drunken uncle would barge in at 2 or 3 in the morning and beat the shit out of everybody, including my father. The cycle of violence then continued on to us. He was very troubled but I couldn't figure out why. This gave me a better understanding of him. He told me that he escaped to Poland because he got a scholarship there, but I don't know if that was the truth or he was just saying that. There, he'd meet my mother in Lodz.

Back in Ecuador when his father died, he never left a will, and so what ended up happening was that his greedy aunts divided the money amongst themselves, leaving nothing for my father and my uncle. They opened jewelry and clothing stores, sent their kids to the finest private schools.

Deep down, my father resented his family and his mother. The problem was that my father had a lot of money and couldn't crossover to America with over $20,000 in his bank account because customs could seize it and question it. And so, my abuelita told him that she would hold it for him, but she bought with it plane tickets for her other nieces and nephews to Florida, and later when he asked for the money back she gave him back only $18,000, and told him that the $2000 was taxes that he had to pay her for her holding his money. My father was a good guy at heart I realized, but he was troubled. The same charming guy who fought for me after a man sold me a used Motorola cell phone that didn't work was the same guy who'd violently yell and scare the shit out of not only me, but other people. I remember one day water was leaking through our walls and my mother asked the upstairs neighbor to not use her water. But she kept using it. My father went up there and my father yelled in a very violent way and said some pretty nasty things to our upstairs neighbor to the point where everyone in the building heard him, and the woman's 2 sons wanted to beat up my father for what he did. My father was a mysterious man, with a heart of gold and a troubled mind. Back to the story.

Basically the apartment that my grandmother gave us was her niece's apartment, but her niece moved out and it should've been ours. And so even though we had lived there, my abuelita never saw it as my father's apartment. My aunt would come whenever she pleased and ask to use the bathroom but my mother wouldn't let her in. These people were fucking assholes and my grandmother put my father through a lot. I remember one time she presented me with a

Super Soaker and then wanted to charge me for it! The nerve! These were the kinds of things that my grandma would do. Another time we went to Hoboken, New Jersey for to celebrate Christmas with some other aunts, and my grandmother bought everyone presents except for me and my brother. When asked why she did that, she said, "I thought you bought them presents." Later, when we moved to Colorado, my father would rent out the apartment to German students. At first everything was fine, but my grandmother began telling them supposed things that my father said to insult them, and one day she told a black student who lived at that apartment that my father was racist and called her bad names. The black student got upset, and she decided not to send the rent checks to my father anymore, and he wasn't getting paid. That's the kind of shit that she did, and it was no wonder that my father was all fucked up inside. He was in shock that his own mother did this to him. My father had always told me that the #1 problem in the world was money, and I saw why he believed it so much. For the first time, it all made sense why he was the way he was. There was clarity there that had never been there before. He was extremely frugal with money, and he was very abusive, and I began to see that I should practice forgiveness, because although it was his choice to abuse us, it wasn't entirely his fault.

I always idolized my grandmother. She was a true hustler who worked for Pierre Cardin as a janitor and when they threw out shoes she'd go get them and fix them up and sell them. She hustled unlike anyone I had ever known. She'd make delicious Ecuadorian chicken soup and sell them for $3 a cup, and she worked two jobs. She had a couple of condos in Florida and bought my cousins all a condo. But in the end we spoke, and when I asked her why she bought everyone a condo except my brother and I, she said, I'm not getting you a condo. I finally began to see that what my father was saying was true. She was evil. One day, she called me because my father exploded on her because they were arguing about money and she wouldn't pay the cell phone bill that he'd been paying for her, instead she told him, "Take it out of what you owe me."

I don't know all the details all I know was that money caused that whole family to divide. And they didn't include my father when they divided up the money and it really hit him hard. I felt sympathy for him for the first time in my life. But he could still be an asshole, and it seemed like life just flew by so fast, the man who I once thought of as Superman and my idol, was now an old man. The man who would yell and critique me, was now asking for help with rides to BJ's. I had to help them, only because I knew they didn't have a car and I somewhat felt that it was my obligation to help my parents out. I mean, they did give me life.

PANDEMIC 2020

During February of 2020, the Coronavirus Pandemic hit. At first, I was panicking about touching anything because of germs. It was also scary to see that there was no one on the streets. I tried to shoot some hoops before they tied up the hoops and made it a rule that no one was to be out playing basketball. The worst part of it all, was that gyms were closed, and that was how I took out my anxiety. So what did we do? We took rides to my storage unit in Weymouth and picked out movies to watch, we often found solace and serenity in hiking-we did that a lot. But I'm not gonna lie it was hard. Hard to watch the news and see the lack of facemasks and other PPE equipment for doctors and nurses. It made me really appreciate all of the frontline workers, It was sad to see that if you were dying or had Corona your own family and friends couldn't see you at the hospital, you just died there...

Times were crazy and what was even more strange was that right before COVID hit, we were in New York City, at the Hilton in Times Square. I took Erika on a vacation, but I was really there to attend a famous producer's studio workshop. The producer was none other than hip hop's Greg Arsonist of the Heatmakerz. He was a cool dude, I found him a little bit arrogant but he was okay. I'll never forget how many talented people I saw there, a couple of them tried to slide him demo tapes and things of that nature. Anyway, at the end of the workshop, came in Fred Da Godson, who was one of the up and coming rappers from the Bronx. He was obese and didn't look like he exercised or took care of himself much. But I'll never forget when he walked up to me and said, "What up boy?" and gave me daps. He was a nice guy, and a couple of weeks later he actually ended up dying from COVID. It was so sad to see that people were dying left and right at a rapid rate, and I really saw how much our country began to work together-people were helping out wherever they could, and that made me feel good.

HOUSING IN YARMOUTH
MAY 2020

I continued to live with Erika, for a little over a year, when I received an offer for state housing in Yarmouth. This was in beautiful Cape Cod, and I felt like I needed a new beginning, and so I accepted. It felt bittersweet moving from Quincy only because I'd be so far away from the friends I met there and Erika.

I spent 1 year alone there, and I'd become a drunk, buying $200 worth of alcohol weekly and drinking every day. The thing is, I feel that my parents influenced me to go on SSDI, or disability at such a young age, but it was the wrong thing to do...Why? Simply because, society does not give two fucks about the disabled or the elderly. The community that I lived in felt like a ghost town. Nobody was happy, and it seemed like they were all just waiting to die. This wasn't the environment for me, I needed to be out keeping busy. I had dreams and goals and was extremely ambitious, and I knew that I had to get out of this life.

This was around the time that Erika bought me a Tesla. I was the only one in public housing, with an expensive electric sports car parked there! It was insane. We ended up getting rid of the car and trading it in for a brand new Toyota Rav4 Hybrid, and it was the first time in my life that I had bought a new car. The Tesla, however, was still a crazy and once in a lifetime experience.

MCLEAN DETOX

In July of 2020, I tried to help myself by admitting myself at the Detox Program at McLean Hospital. I chose Mclean because it was the #1 hospital for psychiatry in the world, and my time there was excellent. I met a couple of really cool people, and the groups that we did helped a lot. I openly spoke about my struggles with alcohol, and how it really began to get worse after I was told to take a year off of social work school. I spoke to one of the counselors who gave me this advice, he told me to go back and finish school, you owe it to yourself. It felt really good to hear someone rooting and believing in me. I remember my father telling me that he didn't believe in me, and that just crushed me.

The detox program lasted for 1 week, and I enjoyed it. I remember getting out, and just taking in the fresh air, and the sunshine. I was happy to be out. Although I built somewhat of a support system with my friends Rob and Tom, I realized that I didn't have my recovery tools that I needed. I didn't participate in groups such as AA, and this was a big mistake.

In January of 2021, I decided that enough was enough, and I applied for fulltime work after 8 years of being on disability. The problem with being on this is that it keeps you in poverty for the rest of your life. I made $1300 a month, half of that went to pay the rent! I barely had enough to live off of and had to get food stamps to stay afloat. Simply put, the system was set against us. And so it was up to me to get out of poverty, and so I began working for rich people as a caregiver for their autistic teens. I thrived on this for a while, and made some decent money, but deep down I worried that I'd get caught. Anyway, in January I applied fulltime to a homeless shelter and got the job. I was transitioning to work, and it wasn't easy at first socializing with people. I was extremely anxious and shy. I wouldn't speak in groups and this was hurting me. Later, in April, I'd get a job as a Mental Health Worker II and work for the State of Massachusetts. I took it and began working both jobs.

One of the most important things that I did was began to care about myself more, and practiced self care. I began working out everyday once the gyms opened up, and in May of 2021, I knew that if I didn't stop drinking that my liver and kidneys would shit the bed and I would die a painful death. My team of doctors tried to warn me to stop immediately, but I didn't listen to them. I had to hit rock bottom to see for myself that the negative patterns that I was habitually practicing weren't healthy, and so I quit drinking. I called my PCP and asked her to prescribe me Campral. I had some friends from the program who were on it and absolutely loved it. It had worked for them. At first, they wanted to put me on Antabuse, but I heard that if you drank one sip, or even applied a spray of cologne, that you'd get really really sick and would have to go to the ER. So I didn't take the prescribed Antabuse. I didn't really quit drinking until almost a full year later.

PRESENT DAY

I learned that we cannot change the past, but we can change our present situation. I was drinking because I was angry and resentful as well as felt like a failure and shamed for most of my life, but I realize that only I can fix my situation and make the pain go away. Was I traumatized from my crazy life? Of course I was. I could play the victim all my life or I could be the best version of me that I could. I also learned that you are who you are, and you're unique and special and nobody has the right to treat you with less respect because of your quirks and mannerisms. Was it hard to accept myself? Hell yea! Because for the longest time I hated who I was and I couldn't accept myself-I had severe anxiety, a mood disorder and apparently everything else under the sun. It wasn't pretty. But I had to learn to overcome it. I had to learn that I have a severe mental illness and unfortunately there is no cure for it- but there is treatment, with the help of antipsychotic meds and mood stabilizers along with Cognitive Behavioral Therapy and a structured schedule you CAN get better. I learned that since Bipolar disorder is not curable practicing self care daily is extremely important. And as far as being shy to this day I'm shy, the only difference is I accept it as part of my personality. If you think about it, there's nothing wrong with being an introvert, as long as you accept yourself. What isn't okay was that severe anxiety and nervousness I used to have, and couldn't control. That is something that may be part of your personality, but with the right medication and tools it can be controlled.

Bullying someone because they are different is never okay, but I've learned that the longer you hold grudges it does nothing but make you worse. The key is to forgive those who trespass against you, that's how you set free what was bothering you for so long. I've forgiven all the people in my life that have done me wrong, not for their sake, but fore mine. I feel like they didn't know any better. We were all young, and it's not fair to be resentful of what happened so long ago. We were all teenagers with our own problems and others had problems we knew nothing about, and so, shit happens. I want anyone who is in high school and is a teenager and reading this and hating high school because of the bullies and all of that to know- don't be afraid to reach out for help. I didn't, and it only made matters worse for me. I don't mean to sound like Ms. Aguilera, but you ARE beautiful, and rest assured, there is life after high school and it does get better. One thing though that I realized that I didn't have was resources to reach out. You see, when I was growing up and in high school we didn't have the resources that are available to teens today. I work as a volunteer for Crisis textline, and I find this an invaluable tool to help teens or anyone that needs it really. Never forget who you are, and don't be afraid to reach out for help.

All we can do in life is to be a good person, treat other people fairly and with respect, and always try to stay optimistic through whatever you're dealing with.

As for my father, the same person who did all that to me throughout my life, I've learned that people are who they are because we are all a product of our environment. I learned that my father also did not have an easy life, and he still to this day does and say things that bother me. I visit them once or twice a month, they live in Dorchester in the Savin Hill area, where I drive them to Costco and help them with groceries because they don't have a car. Inter-generational abuse is a vicious cycle, and It's my job going forward that I cut that cycle of abuse. It's up to me, and no one else...

My father is an old man now, can you believe that I was terrified of this man for all these years? If you're reading this dad, you were always my hero, my Superman. You were always the person that I both feared and idolized...you were always a mysterious and difficult figure that I could never understand, but life changes us and as we grow older we begin to see things more clearly. So father, if you're reading this, it took me a long time to heal, I'm still not fully there yet, but I have the strength and the courage to say that I forgive you.

~The End~

www.ingramcontent.com/pod-product-compliance
Lightning Source LLC
Chambersburg PA
CBHW011147290426
44109CB00023B/2522